RELEVANT LITURGY

Relevant Liturgy

ZABRISKIE LECTURES 1964

L. W. Brown

Archbishop of Uganda and Rwanda-Urundi

New York
Oxford University Press
1965

Printed in Great Britain by
The Camelot Press Ltd., London and Southampton

BV
10
.2
B7

Contents

Acknowledgements

Thanks are due to the following for permission to quote from copyright material:

The Christian Theological Seminary, Indianapolis, Indiana: reprint from *Encounter*, vol. 24, no. 3 of an article by Professor Watkins.

The editor of *Studia Liturgica:* reprint of an article entitled "The Origin of the Church's Liturgy", by Massey H. Shepherd, Jr.

Faber and Faber Ltd: Apostle and Bishop, by A. G. Hebert.

Thomas Nelson and Sons Ltd: *The Revised Standard Version of the Bible*, copyrighted 1946 and 1952.

Oliver and Boyd Ltd: *Eucharist and Sacrifice*, by G. Aulen.

Oxford University Press: Liturgy of the Church of South India.

The Protestant Episcopal Theological Seminary: reprint from the *Seminary Journal*, July 1964, of an article by John H. Rodgers.

S.C.M. Press, Augsburg Publishing House, and World Council of Churches: *Faith and Order Findings—the Report of the Fourth World Conference on Faith and order*, edited by Paul S. Minear.

S.C.M. Press, Association Press, and World Council of Churches: *Fourth World Conference on Faith and Order*, edited by P. C. Rodger and L. Vischer.
S.C.M. Press and Seabury Press: *Local Church and World Mission*, by Douglas Webster.

S.C.M. Press: *Symbolism in the Bible and the Church*, by G. Cope.

Seabury Press: reprint from *Liturgy is Mission*, edited by F. S. Cellier, of an article entitled "Liturgy and Mission", by Massey H. Shepherd, Jr.

Sheed and Ward Ltd: *The Living Church*, by Hans Kung.

The Synod of Bishops of the Church of the Province of South Africa: The South African Prayer Book.

Whitegate Publications: *Constitution on the Sacred Liturgy*, Vatican Council, 1963.

The 1662 Book of Common Prayer of the Church of England is Crown copyright, and the extracts herein are reproduced by permission.

Foreword

These lectures were delivered in the Protestant Episcopal Seminary, Alexandria, Virginia, in April 1964 at the invitation of the Dean, the Very Reverend Jesse Trotter, and are printed in more or less the form in which I gave them.

The few days I spent in Virginia Seminary were extremely happy and I wish to express my deep gratitude to the Faculty and the Student Body for their friendship and patience. The Seminary is making a big contribution to the life of the Church of Uganda in various ways and for that also we are very grateful.

LESLIE, ARCHBISHOP OF UGANDA

1

The Nature of Liturgy

INTRODUCTION

A word of explanation and apology is perhaps necessary before I start my lectures. A man who has been called to a full-time ministry of study and teaching might be far more competent to deal with the subject of Relevant Liturgy than I am. Since the beginning of 1938 I have been serving outside my own country and in conditions which have denied me access to most writing on this subject in America and Europe. What I have to say comes from general experience of the pastoral ministry and from two particular jobs I have had to do as part of that ministry.

At the first Synod of the Church of South India in 1948 I was chosen as Convenor of the Liturgy Committee. There was at that time no intention to prepare new forms of service for the newly united Church, but the unity we were given after Union overruled that intention. Members of a Diocesan Council brought up in different traditions wanted to share in the Eucharist when they met, but they did not want to celebrate the Eucharist according to their previous partial denominational tradition, and within a few months the Liturgy Committee was commissioned by the Synod Executive to draw up a new form of service for Holy Communion. Thus I was thrown right into the stream of liturgical renewal. The result of our work was the Liturgy of the Church of South India.

A somewhat similar need has been felt in Africa where extremes of churchmanship are represented in the Anglican Provinces. A rite which would follow the lines laid down by Lambeth in 1958 and would serve as an instrument of unity has been called for, and I was asked to organize the compilation of such a liturgy.

My lectures to you on Relevant Liturgy can make no pretence to academic excellence or to originality of thought, but they come out of the experience of trying to help meet the pastoral situation of which I have told you.

It is my intention to speak first about the nature of Christian liturgy and then to go on in the second lecture to consider what must be done to show that liturgy is relevant to our contemporary world. In the third lecture I wish to examine the Report of the Committee on the Prayer Book in the 1958 Lambeth Conference, the Report on Worship accepted by the Fourth World Conference on Faith and Order held in Montreal in July 1963, and the Constitution on the Sacred Liturgy promulgated by the Vatican Ecumenical Council on 4 December 1963. I think that this examination shows a very great measure of agreement among all Christian people on the purpose and nature of the liturgy. It is important to know that the Orthodox Church was strongly represented at Montreal, together with the other non-Roman Catholic Confessions belonging to the World Council.

In my fourth lecture I hope to show how this agreement and these convictions which are now so widely held have been embodied in an actual eucharistic rite. Here I want to explain the Liturgy for Africa, with a good many glances at the Liturgy of the Church of South India.

The Text on which I want to speak is contained in the Report of Section IV of the Montreal Conference entitled *The Nature of Christian Worship*.

We believe that Christian worship is deeply relevant to the daily life of men in this present age. At the same time, we realize that the liturgical forms and language of the churches, including that of preaching, are everywhere in need of transformation. In both respects, we, who have come together from all parts of the world and from virtually all the prominent traditions of the Church, have reached what is to us a remarkable consensus. We have found much agreement on what constitutes Christian worship and upon the value of the particular emphases which each of our liturgical traditions has contributed.

2

Yet we have also been compelled to agree that these traditions are inadequate for the current mission of the Church. A proper indication of this consensus is scarcely possible within the allotted scope of this report. However, we believe we can point to a certain direction in which the Spirit may be moving the Churches to-day.[1]

Here are two points which bring into focus and relation the main theses I shall put before you. First, the belief that Christian worship is deeply relevant to the daily life of men and that the expressions of worship must be such that the relevance will be clearly seen and felt by men of to-day. Secondly, the remarkable agreement among the Churches about the nature of Christian worship and the importance of this agreement in realizing, making visible and actual, the unity of the whole Christian Church.

I use the word "liturgy" to mean a form of corporate worship, except when I speak of "the liturgy", when I follow the Orthodox and Anglican usage to mean "eucharistic worship in its fullest sense: i.e. the act of worship of the assembled people of God, of which the Sacrament of the Eucharist forms the centre, but which includes the reading of the Scriptures, the proclamation of the Gospel, the intercessory prayers, the confession of faith, and the praise of the Lord as well".[2]

1

Twenty years ago I was speaking about the study of liturgy to a bishop who was a good theologian. His remarks were almost scornful. He implied that anyone with a smattering of historical knowledge about early liturgy could be reckoned an expert, as few people had time to waste on the subject. Liturgics was reckoned to be either a purely historical study, or a cramming of facts about the Book of Common Prayer into the minds of

[1] *Report of Section IV*, Montreal 1963, para. 105. (This document is referred to hereafter as *Section IV Report*.)
[2] *Report on Worship*, Montreal 1963, p. 16. (Referred to hereafter as *Report*.)

3

ordinands. In the last twenty years, much new work has been done. The most ancient forms of Christian Worship have been sought out and compared with each other and much is known about the sources of Christian worship. It is, of course, quite necessary to study liturgy in this manner, but it can be a deadening occupation. It is necessary to see what cultural and theological factors influence the form of any liturgy, but liturgy is fundamentally not a form of words to be studied but the activity of a living body. It is not possible fully to understand its meaning and purpose by dissecting the prayers; you have to enter into the life of the living body, using the form, if you are really to understand and appreciate its importance. *Liturgy is primarily the means by which God is believed to communicate with his people and to speak his word; it is also the response of God's people to what he says.* I like very much the Vatican Council's definition:

> Although the sacred liturgy is above all things the worship of the divine Majesty, it likewise contains much instruction for the faithful. For in the liturgy God speaks to his people and Christ is still proclaiming his gospel. And the people reply to God both by song and prayer.[1]

If you accept these definitions of the purpose of liturgy, then that word can be used only in connection with theistic worship. Gifts to the spirits or the technique of divination cannot be dignified with the word liturgy, although it was precisely in this context of performing rites necessary to secure the favour of the unseen spiritual forces for the whole community that the word liturgy received a cultic meaning in Greek and Roman times. (The word originally seems to have meant any work done by a citizen as part of his duty to the State.)

In these early dealings of man with spiritual powers, whether we examine them in the paganism of the Graeco-Roman world or in the "primal vision" of African culture, the main emphasis does seem to be on divine communication and human response.

[1] *Constitution on the Sacred Liturgy*, Vatican Council 1963, 33. (Hereafter referred to as *Constitution*.)

4

Divination is practised by means of people who become possessed with a spirit invading them from outside, or the divine intention is sought for by lots or by augury of various kinds. But man's response to this is not one of praise and adoration; it is of gifts of sacrifice to put right his inadvertent errors, whether of omission or commission. There is no expectation of a revelation of God's will and nature, nor of a challenge to moral decision and obedience.

For us Christians, God who spoke of old to our fathers by the prophets in many and various ways has in these last days spoken to us by a Son (Heb. 1.1,2). His word to man is clear and definite, because he became incarnate.

> The decisive event of the death and resurrection of Jesus Christ as the culmination of the mighty saving acts of God forms the living centre of all worship, and the Holy Spirit is the energy which creates and preserves it.[1]

Christian worship is thus centred on the action of God which was accomplished once for all in human history at a certain place and time in Jesus Christ our Lord, but which is also a contemporary and present act by the power of the Holy Spirit working in his people, through which Christ is still alive in our hearts through faith. The core of Christian worship is thus something given, unchanging and unchangeable, relevant for all people at all times and in all places. Liturgy is the proclamation of this revelation.

But the manner in which this central and directive truth is presented must be relevant and intelligible to men in every age and in every place. The bare words of the Creed, "He suffered under Pontius Pilate", are not enough. The meaning and significance of the historic event recalled by those words must be shown. When we try to describe significance and spiritual value, we are at once committed to the use of language different from the language ordinary people in our western civilization use to describe the things that interest them. We live in a technical and scientific age and our language reflects this. We use factual description. When

[1] *Report*, pp. 10, 11.

we express appreciation, it is usually for the usefulness or ingenuity of a product—we do not usually react in terms of unsophisticated wonder, because we know that, if we take the trouble to understand, we can probably understand how a thing works, and then it seems there is no place for wonder. But we cannot use scientific language for spiritual description, we have to use the language of poetry, of myth—parable, allegory, metaphor, simile.

The Bible is written in such language, and when it was written the figures it employs were intelligible to the people for whom it was written and to whom the prophecies were spoken. When the Book of Jonah was written, probably no one who read it thought it described an actual unfortunate occurrence in which a man was swallowed by a great fish. It was immediately understood as a picture of the great Empire of Assyria swallowing up and destroying the little nation of Israel, and as a pledge that even though Israel appeared to die, God would bring it to life again because of his faithfulness and love. Perhaps certain Christian sects might not have had so much self-righteous indignation against the Roman Church if they had understood a little more about the scarlet woman. The author of the Apocalypse used the Old Testament experience of Babylon as the empire which persecuted the people of God, the very embodiment of human pride and self-sufficiency, to expose the Roman Empire which was going exactly the same way. The scarlet woman is a picture of all human systems which regard man and man's wisdom as self-sufficient, and which, therefore, regard Christians who have an other-worldly reference as potentially subversive and dangerous. Perhaps I need not point out that in these days the Church in many places still lives with this problem. It is our inability to obey the State with no reservations at all which makes us objects of suspicion. In countries with authoritarian régimes the Church lives through the first three centuries again, every day.

One of the most pressing needs of our day is for the Church really to understand what God is saying through the Bible. Modern scholarship has illumined the meaning of biblical language in a

6

wonderful way, but the new knowledge has not yet reached most Church members. The vast majority of Christians are probably unconscious fundamentalists. In the younger Churches of Africa and Asia, children who begin to learn elementary science see at once a contradiction to the literal meaning of the scriptural words. They have never been taught what the Bible is really saying about God and man, and so the vast majority of them dismiss the Bible as untrue. They have learned stories, not their meaning, and they dismiss them as irrelevant, stories for ignorant children but not for educated people.

Here is one of the most urgent tasks of the Church, to find intelligible language to proclaim the biblical revelation, language which will clearly show the acts of God in Christ to be meaningful and relevant not only to the needs of the individual but to the community and to mankind as a whole. We need a "rebirth of images". We have to examine the images we currently use, to reject images which are misleading, to offer a reinterpretation and re-presentation of the once-for-all events, the core of liturgy, in a form understood by the people. Some kind of demythologization and remythologization is essential for evangelism to-day, and as essential for relevant liturgy.

Here we touch the whole problem of indigenization. When the Gospel goes to Africa or Asia it must be expressed in words which are intelligible and relevant.

Indigenization of the Christian way of life, in every country to which the gospel comes, is a natural corollary to the doctrine of the Incarnation, according to which God not only became man, but expressed that manhood in terms of the time and place in which he lived. His birth into a Jewish home placed him in a particular context in the history of God's chosen people to whom are called people of all nations to which the gospel comes. Indigenization is, therefore, a process by which the life of Christ expresses itself in the members of his Body, in the several regional churches.

Also indigenization may be understood as another aspect of identification. This principle also provides a warning against

7

wrong types of indigenization. Patterns of worship should be relevant for the life of the people. For example, in a congregation of an urban or industrial background, symbols taken from a purely rural setting can be as artificial and unnatural as the continuance of the alien patterns . . . indigenization cannot be achieved merely as a human contrivance. It is what the Church evolves when guided by the Holy Spirit, who continually revives the Church and sustains it as the Body of Christ.[1]

There can easily be attempts at surface indigenization which are misleading and dangerous. A man from outside a culture may think he recognizes certain symbols or art forms in it as akin to his own Christian concepts or experience, and press on the indigenous Christian community the use of these familiar symbols. Often they will reject them, as, for example, most African Christians reject music and dances with a pagan origin. They know better than the outsider the emotional and mythic content of these symbols, and they refuse to confuse the old and the new. This difficulty is not new—the writers of Alexandria and men like Tertullian did not agree on the question of whether non-Christian approach to God was inspired by the Word, the light that lighteth every man, or was to be rejected as a counterfeit of the devil.

A very wise word comes from the Japanese Dr Masao Takenaka on this subject:

I am inclined to think that the starting point of the indigenization of Christian faith is not so much in the field of architecture or music or art, not even in theology, but in the field of the Christian style of living in contemporary Asia. Unless we Asian Christian men and women in our ordinary Church life take seriously the responsibility to wrestle with common problems in the ordinary life of Asian society, there will be no spontaneous expression of indigenous Christian faith. If a man is deeply rooted in Christ and deeply rooted in Asian soil, no matter how insignificant and small he be, he magnifies a radiating example of the indigenization of Christianity, simply by being what he is. Through the searching question coming out of the struggling experience in secular participation,

[1] *Report*, p. 38.

8

theologians will develop deeper and more penetrating theological formulations in the Asia situation. From the struggling of this rhythmic life rooted both in Christ and in Asian soil there will come a spontaneous expression in songs and art forms expressing joy and thankfulness for his suffering yet victorious ministry. Indigenization will arise from within, in this sense, from the process of the wrestling participation of God's people in the present concrete reality of Asian society.[1]

The life of an African saint like our Canon Apolo Kivebulaya of Uganda[2] makes Dr Takenaka's point very clear. Apolo was a young Muslim soldier who was converted and baptized in 1895. Almost immediately afterwards he offered as a teacher, was given a little instruction, and sent off, two hundred miles away, to another country and tribe. He could not keep silent about his Lord. He pressed on, across the Ruwenzori Mountains to the unknown and feared peoples living in the Ituri Forest in what is now the Republic of the Congo. Apolo identified himself with the people he was preaching to, sleeping on the ground and eating the game and roots on which the pygmies and other people of the forest lived. He was a simple man, with little education, but his own life, rooted in Christ and expressive of him in all he did, showed a true indigenization. It was effected by the Holy Spirit making Christ's revelation the all-sufficient source of life to him, and his own expression of this experience in language and life natural to him. Nobody could possibly have thought that the religion of Apolo Kivebulaya was a foreign thing. It wholly belonged to him and was a life more than a theory. Much the same was true of Sadhu Sundar Singh in India. It seems that indigenization cannot be hurried or forced. It must be the fruit of a life lived in Christ, by the community and the individual, and then it will be authentic and genuine.

This problem is a difficult one and presses on anyone who works in a culture not his own. But, of course, the problem of indigenization presses, in fact, on every Christian, because the new technical

[1] Quoted in *Report*, p. 39.
[2] Anne Luck, *African Saint*, S.C.M. Press, 1963.

culture which has spread over the world in our century has few points of contact with the world of the Bible. With the spread of education even tribal and local cultures in many parts of the world are losing much of their hold on people, unless they are deliberately boosted and employed in the service of nationalism. If Christian faith and worship could be indigenized in the new culture, then it might be seen once more to be a message for the world. If the Christian community hides in a spiritual ghetto, with no communication in spiritual things with its contemporaries with whom it works day by day in office, factory, or laboratory, then the Church is doomed. But if Christians accept the new world culture and, while being in it and part of it, try there to live out and think out the gospel, the Spirit, the Interpreter, will enable us to interpret the old images, and find the new we need.

2

So far I have been speaking of liturgy as the means by which God speaks to his people. The necessity of finding forms through which his word will be made intelligible is clamant. The same considerations hold good if we turn to the other side of liturgy, man's response to God's initiative and God's grace.

Here again, everything that is said and done must be meaningful. Our words and our actions must express what we want to express. For example, take the *Kyrie eleison*, "Lord, have mercy", which we often use in Anglican liturgy. I suppose that the expression probably originated in some oriental court. It may have been a greeting to the monarch, the lord, an acknowledgement of his power, and it seems that this meaning still attached to the words when they made their first appearance in the Christian liturgy in the fourth century. This is the reason for my guess. Often I am summoned to the Court of our Kabaka, the King of Buganda. I sit next to the princes of the blood royal and usually there is an old man sitting on the floor next to me. He has a harp, exactly like those you see the ancient Egyptians using in their wall paintings. When the Kabaka says something important drums beat outside and trumpets blow, and the old harpist starts strumming away, singing about the exploits of the King. This seems to me just the atmosphere from which *Kyrie eleison* came. I sometimes wish my friend would come and squat on the altar steps as well and sing of the great things God has done, for his mercy endureth for ever! It was reasonable to use such words with that meaning as the people's response in almost any kind of supplication or litany, but now in English the words convey an element of penitence and abasement that may not have been there at first.

The problem of translation from one geographic language into another is also an extremely acute one. The Eskimos can hardly confess that they have strayed like lost sheep with any real sense of conviction if they have never seen a sheep, and doubtless some of them wonder what the palm branches they will wave in heaven will be like. I know of one diocese where the good bishop, not a native of that country and not gifted with tongues, habitually mispronounced a word in the confirmation prayer, with the result that in the attempt to make language meaningful it became an accepted part of confirmation instruction in his diocese that when the bishop laid his hands on you and called you a monkey he meant you were the servant of God. It was unfortunate that the words for servant and monkey are so similar.

As with language, so with ceremonies. They must be intelligible, or they completely frustrate their purpose. Cranmer had a lot to say about this in the Preface concerning Ceremonies in 1549:

> But what would Saint Augustine have said, if he had seen the Ceremonies of late days used among us; whereunto the multitude used in his time was not be be compared? This our excessive multitude of Ceremonies was so great, and many of them so dark, that they did more confound and darken, than declare and set forth Christ's benefits unto us.

I remember going to a church in England when I was young and seeing the priest turn to the north corner of the church to read the Gospel in a low voice. The whole purpose of this ceremony

11

appeared to be to show that the Gospel was irrelevant and of no importance to the congregation who could neither see nor hear him speak. This was a far cry from the original significance of this ceremony, when in the southern lands (I speak of Europe) the priest turned to the north, to the still unevangelized areas, with the proclamation of the Gospel.

The people must not only understand and mean what they say and do in responding to God; they must also say it as members one of another in the Christian community. This is why there must be opportunity for the whole congregation to take part, and common ceremonial so that all kneel or stand or sit at the same time. Decency and order is necessary for corporateness. The excessive individualism which is seen in many early Communion services in England, when the people come because they like a quiet service and scatter themselves in individuals or couples all over a large church, is theologically wrong. Christian liturgy must be a corporate act. This is still fairly easy to express in a village church in Africa where the buildings are often small and there is still a great sense of corporateness. Here the difficulty is to arouse the need for individual decision and commitment, which is also a necessary response within the inter-dependent unity of the Christian Church.

In Christian worship the whole community must play its part. The liturgy is not the liturgy of the priest like that glaring example of sacerdotalism when a minister offers a long prayer of his own devising and even says the Amen to it by himself. The Vatican Council says:

> Liturgical services are not private functions, but are celebrations of the Church, which is the "Sacrament of unity", namely, the holy people united and ordered under their bishops. Therefore liturgical services pertain to the whole body of the Church; they manifest it and have effects upon it; but they concern the individual members of the Church in different ways, according to their differing rank, office and actual participation.[1]

[1] *Constitution*, 26, 27.

Moreover, the prayers addressed to God by the priest who presides over the assembly in the person of Christ are said in the name of the entire holy people and of all present.[1]

Too often our liturgy has been mostly intellectual. In the Luganda language the common word for worship is *okusoma*, which means "to read", and the services of the first Christians in Uganda were to a large extent reading demonstrations. We have to be careful that in our desire for intelligibility we do not forget that there are other parts of the human personality than the intellectual. It is because our worship has been expressive of only a part of us that other sects have arisen to meet people's needs. In some Pentecostal Churches they sing till they sweat. But let us not consider such expressions of Christian worship completely eccentric. Their very existence is a judgement on the failure of the historic Churches to give satisfactory expression to the response of the whole person to God.

I am not sure how the element of spontaneity can be given place in corporate worship, in liturgy, but I am sure we have to think about this. I call to mind an example of spontaneity which was utterly right liturgically and which still moves me when I recall it. On Christmas Day 1944, I had gone to an outcastes' village built among palm trees almost on the beach of the Indian Ocean in Travancore. There was a great Hindu temple in the near vicinity, and the conversion of these outcastes was not looked on with favour. As outcastes they knew their place in society—they hadn't any place. As Christians they seemed to think they were full men and women. It was probably unwise to build themselves a brick church in such a place, but they did it. Then persecution broke out. The church was wrecked and demolished. Their benches and furniture were broken up. Their palm trees were cut down. Human excrement was thrown in their little houses. The police came and warned them that if they met for worship it would be conduct leading to a breach of the peace and so to criminal action.

[1] *Constitution*, 33.

13

I had not been going to them. White faces would have been a liability to them. But when the last threat came I went. I went on Christmas Day to give them the Lord in the Eucharist. We prayed under the trees, and they had put up a few cheap coloured streamers and stuck red hibiscus flowers on the bushes. They were all there, in their best clothes, even though we knew we might all be stoned or arrested. Before the Prayer for the Church I asked if any of them would like to offer a prayer. One man said, "Lord, we thank you for the message of Christmas, of your birth in a stable. We built you a house, but you can't come there—it is destroyed. But again, where men have refused you a dwelling, you have come to us." That prayer was wholly spontaneous and wholly liturgical too, though it came from a man who had never heard of liturgy and probably could not write his own language. The symbols were full of meaning, they conveyed truth. God spoke to him through them and he was able to respond, along with all his fellows—you should have heard the Amen to that prayer.

Perhaps spontaneity is like true indigenization. It can be present only when the priestly body, the worshippers and their minister, live in the power of the Gospel and so begin to express it naturally in terms of their own age and circumstance. It may be this whole business of making liturgy meaningful and relevant is at heart the old call to more complete consecration and control by God the Holy Spirit.

I wish to enlarge and sum up what I have said in a definition of the nature of Christian worship taken from the Montreal Report:

In Christian worship, God comes to us in Christ through the Holy Spirit, sustains us through his grace, establishes us in fellowship with him and with one another, and empowers us for his service in the world. In worship, we come to God in Christ, the True Worshipper, who by his incarnation, servanthood, obedience unto death, resurrection and ascension, has made us participants in the worship which he offers. In him, truly God, we have access to the Father; in him, truly Man, we are restored to our true nature as worshippers of God. Christian worship is, therefore, a service to God the Father by men redeemed by his Son, who are continually finding new life in the power of the Holy Spirit.

Christian worship, as a participation in Christ's own self-offering, is an act formative of Christian community—an act, moreover, which is conducted within the context of the whole Church, and which represents the one, catholic Church.[1]

[1] *Section IV Report*, 108 (*a*), (*b*).

2

Relevant Liturgy

It is well that I can assume that I am speaking in these lectures to those who believe in God and in his purpose for all mankind. For all others the title I have chosen, Relevant Liturgy, is non-sense. I do not forget that behind all our discussion is a large question-mark in the minds of the great majority of men alive in the world to-day. We say that worship is acknowledgement, but they would say, acknowledging what and to whom? The basic challenge to the Church is in fact man's unbelief, not reform in his way of listening to God or responding to him. However, in this lecture we have to leave this fundamental question. Yet surely we ought never to forget the vast majority of mankind for whom what we do and enjoy in worship is meaningless. One of the factors which ought to influence our worship as well as our theology is the evangelistic motive—so that all we think, say, and do, can commend the truth and love of God to those who do not know him.

I concluded the first lecture with an incident which brought spontaneity and relevance into the Book of Common Prayer Liturgy of 1662, which had been translated into rather clumsy Malayalam and was apparently completely unrelated in its setting to the people and their environment. This was possible because, though the form was inadequate, the content was accepted and understood. My argument is that the central core of liturgy, the Gospel of God and the people's response, does not change, but that the forms of its expression need constant re-formation and revision, so that they present and illuminate the Gospel, instead of hindering and obscuring it. The 1662 Book of Common Prayer, even in its many translations, does preserve and express this central truth, but the language in English is archaic, and the vocabulary quite different from that used in everyday life. This form, appreciated though it may be for the cadences of its language and the majesty of its impression, may easily become an end in itself. "The service was beautifully sung this morning." "Mr so-and-so read the lessons in a most dignified way." Yes. But were the worshippers, conscious of their unity in the Spirit, moved to hear a word of God spoken to their own need and the need of their nation, and strengthened to go into the world as witnesses of the Saviour and living agents of the love of God? Was their liturgy part of all their life, or an irrelevant activity of another kind, not meaningful in the context of the everyday world? Does what we do on Sunday really impinge upon and change what we do on Monday? This surely is a real question.

I think that if we examine the history of Christian worship in the historic Church we can see there have been alternations of mood. There have been periods when the Holy Spirit has so worked in the Church that man's acknowledgement of God in worship became fresh, vivid, and relevant. When these periods have passed, man's conservatism in religious habits has kept the form but often lost the spirit; worship has become fossilized and a manifestation of law until such time as God has woken us again to the reality of his call in the contemporary world. It is really the Reformation slogan *Ecclesia semper reformanda*, which Professor Kung seems now to have claimed for the Roman Catholic Church, which is the truth. Relevance and life come through the energy, the working of the Holy Spirit. It is he who in every generation can take the things of Christ and show them to us. It is he who makes Christ always relevant. He makes all things new, and through him the judgement of the Word on the Church is mediated and applied.

I think that the worship of the first Christians was probably entirely intelligible to them. Those who had been Jews knew the Synagogue service, although the majority of them may have had no direct contact with the sacrificial cult of the Temple. We know

17

that the Jews of the Dispersion and the god-fearers came to Jerusalem for the feasts, but outside Jerusalem the Temple cultus was spiritualized and turned into a type, replaced throughout the dispersed communities by readings and prayers which were rationalized substitutes for sacrifice. Christian worship must have seemed very little different from Jewish worship, except for its triumphant note of the fulfilment of promise. No longer need they long for the promised Messiah. He had come, and was working among them by his Spirit. And this faith illuminated and quickened the whole worship. The prophecies had come alive, the whole Old Testament was seen to speak one thing, and that thing was proclaimed in every Christian sermon—"as he spake by the prophets", "as is written in the Scriptures". In the light of Christ the old symbols were seen to be relevant and cogent, though even they were insufficient to describe the richness of Christ. The Jews believed that the images and pictures used in the Scriptures were given by God himself, they were powerful to convey that which they represented; they were, if you like, sacramental. In Christ, they were fulfilled. He was understood in the light of them—the Vine, the Servant, the Rock, the Son, the Light, the Shepherd—and so the early Christians rejoiced in the freshness and authenticity of their worship. A woman who is a very talented musician was converted some years ago. She said to me after this, radiantly, "I'm hearing all kinds of things now in the music I never knew were there. The whole thing is living." That is how the Bible seemed to the first Christians. The images were manifest; the promises fulfilled.

G. A. F. Knight has set down the interpretation of Israel's history and calling which seems to have been held, at every period, by the writers of the canonical books.[1] God promised the birth of Israel, his servant, and Israel was duly born out of the pain of Egypt and baptized in the Red Sea. Then at Sinai Israel was solemnly married to God, but proved a faithless wife and was

---

[1] G. A. F. Knight, *A Christian Theology of the Old Testament*, London 1959, pp. 202 ff.

justly punished for her sins, died in the destruction of the nation in 587 B.C., was buried, and descended into hell. Then, when all hope in human power or alliances was at an end, God brought the nation back from the dead and the faithful looked forward in hope to a day when the whole cosmos would be reconciled.

Such was the myth of God's action. In the Christ, the Servant of God, the true Israel, all was fulfilled. God's reality and power were clearly seen. He had been born. He had died. All hope had died with him. He had been raised from the dead. Hope was reborn. The Spirit had been poured on all flesh, the dry bones had been quickened, the new Israel, the people of God, had been buried with him in baptism and raised to newness of life. I believe this is how the first Christians of Jewish origin felt their faith. The Old Testament symbols and words became meaningful and contemporary, and the sacraments of Baptism and the Eucharist were the means by which the believer was incorporated into that life of Christ and his Church.

The first pagan converts also found the liturgy of the Christians relevant and intelligible. They too were conscious of living in the experience to which the whole liturgy witnessed. These men and women were drawn at first mostly from the ranks of the god-fearers, the non-Jews who were attached to the synagogues, doubtless attracted by the austerity of Jewish monotheism and its moral demands. They disliked the system of the pagan cult, with its idols, drunken feasts, and prostitution, and its lack of any moral lead; and perhaps they were not sophisticated enough for the alternative, philosophy, and, later, the mystery cults. As god-fearers they knew the meaning of the Old Testament myth. In Christ they who once were far off had become near; those who were not the people of God had become his people; the wall of partition between Jew and Gentile had been broken down in Christ. The worship spoke of and confirmed them in that freedom.

It seems clear from the New Testament that there was no problem of making Christian worship relevant. The Christians understood their acknowledgement of God to be expressed in the

19

obedience of their daily lives. Their meeting for worhip was not different in kind from their fellowship and their discipleship in ethical obedience. In the New Testament there is therefore no vocabulary of worship in the narrow sense. They had no special buildings, no written rites, no order of ministry considered to be parallel to or like the pagan priesthood. Their whole life was centred in the belief that God had acted in Jesus Christ and that they were now living as free and forgiven men in the power of the Holy Spirit. It was essential for them to meet together to praise their Lord and to be renewed in him, so that they might live out a life of moral victory in the world. Their worship was part of this whole life, there was no problem of trying to make it relevant.

Probably the manner of Christian worship was fairly constant throughout all the scattered Churches, but there was certainly no uniformity in the prayers of thanksgiving or the words of the Christian prophets. Gradually, during the first century and a half, the first Christian writings were sorted out and on the Church's presumption of apostolic authorship and therefore apostolic authority, the books of the New Testament became canonical. But during this period the real pagans started coming into the fellowship, and they did not understand and accept the *biblical* doctrine of redemption, of life through death, and that only by the grace of God in Christ. So we see interpretation of the Bible which is interesting, like the Shepherd of Hermas, but misses the the essential point, and yet was accepted as Scripture by some of the most prominent leaders like Irenaeus and Tertullian in his catholic days. We find the Gnostic sects, attracted to Christ, yet finding his Jewish dress barbarous and distressing. So, the movement to spiritualize Christianity starts, and only one section of mankind, the really spiritually minded, could ever grasp it or attain salvation. These Gnostics probably used much of the ordinary form of Christian worship, but imposed a totally differ-ent interpretation on what they said and did from the Christians. Marcion went farther and rejected the Old Testament and most of the New, everything which smacked of Jewishness. "He criticized the Scriptures with a penknife"—I am sure you all remember that memorable remark of Tertullian. Indeed we see an almost total change of atmosphere when the Christian community entered the Greek world. The doctrine of grace in the Apostolic Fathers, as Torrance has shown,[1] is miles away from that dependence on the unchanging purposes of God's goodwill of which we read in the New Testament.

The Christian faith was now challenged on all sides by intellectual ideas. The men and women who were possessed by it and the writings in which the apostolic testimony was enshrined seemed naïve to a degree. You will remember, for example, the young Augustine's disgust with the childish nature of the Scriptures and the kind of Latin they were written in, which he considered an insult to an educated man. So the intellectuals among the new converts tried to explain the Old Testament and the liturgy in the categories of their own way of thinking. It seems that typology was almost universally employed. In the first epistle of Clement, Rahab's action in tying the scarlet cord to her window is explained "as showing that by the blood of our Lord should be redemption to all that believe and hope in God".[2] So, in the Epistle of Barnabas the sacrifice of the red heifer in Numbers 19 is expounded:

Consider how all these things are delivered in a figure for us. This heifer is Jesus Christ; the wicked men that offer it are those sinners who brought him to death. . . . Why was the wool put on a stick? Because the kingdom of Jesus was founded upon the cross. . . . Wherefore these things being thus done are to us indeed evident; but to the Jews they are obscure, because they hearkened not unto the voice of the Lord.[3]

This was an attempt to make the Scriptures, and worship which was centred in the Scriptures, intelligible to men of the time.

[1] T. Torrance, *The Doctrine of Grace in the Apostolic Fathers*.
[2] 1 Clement XII.
[3] G. Cope, *Symbolism in the Bible and the Church*, Epistle of Barnabas, VIII, p. 30.

Typology was an attempt to bring rational meaning out of something which seemed irrational. To be a sound Christian it became necessary to express your faith in accepted forms, and orthodoxy came to mean a correct intellectual understanding and expression of the faith rather than the radiant glory of a new life in Christ.

But, to correct these over-simplified generalizations, I quote Massey Shepherd. He says:

> One must be wary of those judgments passed upon the Catholic Church of the second century that speak of it in terms of decline or a perversion of its pristine gospel, as though only those elements of Christian belief and usage are legitimate which are identifiably Hebraic. The Church valiantly continued the work of reconciliation of the Jew and the Greek, bringing together in a single truth the Word of Scripture and the Logos of philosophy.[1]

Then came A.D. 321. The organized world entered the Church in a big way. The resources of the Public Works Department were mobilized to put up Christian churches which surpassed in splendour the old pagan temples. It was no longer easy in these great buildings to have intimate services of deep fellowship. Many of the people who thronged them had never been in danger for their faith; they had followed the crowd into the Church, they had received instruction and accepted a religion. Christianity had become institutionalized. The Emperor himself went to church and the usage of the Byzantine Empire became adapted to Christian worship. The incense burnt before a great officer of the empire as he went through the smelly streets of a city, the staff carried before him on which he leant during long sessions at court, the richness of his clothing, all these became associated with the bishops and priests of the Church. The leaning-staff became a shepherd's crook in the West, and in the East developed into serpents on a pole. Incense, lights, rich vestments, all became symbols of ecclesiastical rank. But their origin was in the secular life of the Empire. Many of the multitude who thronged the

[1] M. H. Shepherd, "The Origin of the Church's Liturgy" in *Studia Liturgica* I.2., June 1962, pp. 88, 89.

churches were not baptized, they went to church because the, Emperor and the Court went. So, the liturgy became a spectacle, continually being improved aesthetically, visually, and audibly but with Communion of the people becoming more and more infrequent, until it became normal, in both East and West, for non-clerics to communicate only once a year.

Yet the liturgy, elaborate though it became in its ceremonial and complex in its ritual, was still developing on its original lines. The Scriptures, however difficult to understand, were still the sacred oracles of God, and great preachers, Augustine, Chrysostom, and others, expounded them. The Church's year, and the Church's week, still centred on the mystery of Christ's death and resurrection, which was the theme of the great anaphoras. These still kept to the fundamental plan and purpose of the ancient Jewish blessings of God, thanksgiving for creation and redemption. Every generation of Christians continued to sing the praises of God in the Psalms. There can be no doubt that this was an age of faith, even if the development of its expression would probably have confused the apostles of the Lord. The fight with rationalism was still on, and elaborations in the baptismal confessions, the creeds, and in the text of the liturgy, were largely in defence of the catholic faith. So also was the choice of the day of Sol Invictus, the winter solstice, to commemorate the birth of the Lord, God from God, Light from Light. It was a direct answer to paganism.

The newly popular religion was certainly not peripheral to life, but how far it had lost its sense of personal relation to the living Saviour and Lord, and the power of bringing men and women to new life in him, is a matter of question. Christ, as the Byzantines later pictured him, sitting on an emperor's throne reigning over the universe, seems at first different from the Jesus of Galilee. The fierce and prolonged controversy about theological definitions seems far removed from the calm simplicity of the Sermon on the Mount. You probably remember Gregory of Nyssa describing the situation in Constantinople:

Why! to-day there are men, like those Athenians, who "spend their time in nothing else but either to tell or to hear some new thing", men of yesterday and the day before, mere mechanics, off-hand dogmatists in theology, servants too and slaves that have been flogged, runaways from servile work, and are solemn with us and philosophical about things incomprehensible. You know quite well to whom I refer. With such the whole city is full; its smaller gates, forums, squares, thoroughfares; the clothes-vendors, the money-lenders, the victuallers. Ask about pence, and he will discuss the Generate and the Ingenerate. Enquire the price of bread, he answers: Greater is the Father, and the Son is subject. Say that a bath would suit you, and he defines that the Son is made out of nothing![1]

Liturgy in the Roman Empire of the fourth century was of a piece with the organization of everyday life—at least in so far as everyday life throughout the tribes of the Empire was marked by those who governed it and their system of government. It had little in common with the simplicity of its origins in the house-churches of the early Christians, but it did belong to the world of everyday life. Its ceremonial expression belonged to, it was not alien to, that world. The non-government Churches outside the Empire, like Persia and its daughter Church of Malabar, also had elaborate ceremonial, not indeed as splendid as those which developed in State-supported basilicas, but still a long way from the simplicity of the worship-gatherings of the first Christians.

"Since the sixth century", as Massey Shepherd says in the article I have quoted,[2] "there has been no major creative development of the liturgy. The history of the Church's liturgical worship has been one of successive and variant periods of elaboration, revision, deformation and recovery." The periods of recovery have, I think, been periods when spiritual renewal has come to the Church or a part of it, as at the time of the Reformation, and this has always been connected with a recovery of biblical theology.

Perhaps liturgy was also intelligible and relevant in the Middle

[1] Gregory, Bishop of Nyssa, 372–95, *De deitate Filii et Spiritus sancti Oratio*, Op. iii 466 D; *P.G.* xlvi. 557 B.
[2] M. H. Shepherd, *The Origin of the Church's Liturgy*, p. 99.

Ages when the concept of Christendom was accepted and was a fact in the West. But probably at most periods liturgical worship was accepted as a duty to be performed, the necessary condition for a peaceful life and prosperous crops. I venture to guess that at most ages and for most people liturgy meant very much what it has meant down the centuries to the St Thomas Christians of Malabar, in South India. Whatever may be the truth of this Church's claim to apostolic origin, by the fifth century they were ruled by the Nestorian Patriarch of Babylon. Then the Portuguese established Roman supremacy among the Indian Christians at the beginning of the sixteenth century, and romanized the ancient Liturgy of Addai and Mari which the Indian Christians were using. But at the turn of that century a Jacobite bishop reached Malabar and about half the Church defected from Rome and joined him, only realizing that the faith of their new pastor was different from that of their former Patriarchs when he celebrated the Liturgy of St James. The words of the Liturgy were unintelligible, being in Syriac as Addai and Mari had been, but he did things in a slightly different way and that betrayed him! In the last thirty or forty years priests have begun to celebrate the liturgy in the local language, Malayalam, but it is not yet universally the case. Throughout the centuries, then, from the fourth century until to-day, the Christian liturgy has been celebrated in a language no layman knew, with the most solemn ceremonies conducted behind a curtain, out of sight of the congregation, with no reading of the Scriptures in the vernacular. It can hardly be said that the liturgy was relevant, it was certainly not intelligible. Yet God used it to symbolize and express the mystery of our redemption, and a living tradition of Christian faith and morals was maintained and passed on.

The situation in medieval Europe was hardly different. Most of the people knew no Latin, their rôle at the Eucharist was that of spectators. Private Masses became common and the Canon was said in silence, and most Christians did not make their Communion more than once a year, if then, judging by the Lateran

Council's attempt in 1215 to enforce that minimum. By the same Council, dogmatic and ceremonial changes were made which could not have been passed had the apostolic practice and tradition in the Scriptures still been the yardstick of true development.

At the time of the Reformation a deliberate attempt was made by the leading reformers to go back to the New Testament norm of worship. In spite of their own background of medieval thought and devotional experience formed by medieval Roman worship, a great many things were done which were revolutionary and were not simply an archaeological attempt to recover an earlier and more primitive way of worship and life. The minister still had as central a position in conducting the liturgy as the priest of the Catholic Church, but in spite of this, Calvin in Geneva and Cranmer in England tried (but failed) to make a weekly Communion of the whole Christian people the norm. The Scriptures and services were translated into the vernacular languages, and not translated into some special ecclesiastical form of the language but into the language of contemporary speech. In England drastic simplifications were made, with the express intention of enabling the whole congregation to join in the whole worship.

From the Reformation until now the Book of Common Prayer has been the basic liturgy of English people. (I hope this does not sound arrogant. I am well aware of the worship of the Non-conforming Churches in England, and I do not discount their influence at all, but I think my remark is true.) The special circumstances of the Episcopal Church in Scotland gave them freedom to draw up their own rite (1637), and the Prayer Book of the Protestant Episcopal Church of the United States of America owes a good deal to it, perhaps again because of the conservatism and legal-mindedness of certain English bishops. But in large parts of our Communion 1662 is still regarded as the Prayer Book, and even in the Provinces which have authorized their own books one usually finds the basis in 1662, tailored to local taste. I am the last man to decry the merits of that great book. I knew no other from my infancy, and my fathers before me were nourished on it. But, in spite of the affection and admiration we have for it, is it really relevant liturgy in twentieth-century England or anywhere else? I cannot think so. Much of its language is incomprehensible, and one cannot truly say that to be saved one needs to understand an archaic vocabulary. It is the living Lord who saves by incorporating us into his mystery. Some of the services, like that of Infant Baptism, convey a very confused meaning, and in many services the element of praise and the opportunity for full congregational participation are lacking.

One of the greatest difficulties about liturgical revision is people's conservatism in matters of worship. It is seen in every aspect of it—architecture, music, words, dress. I like Massey Shepherd's comment on this:

> There is a danger, too, of divisive tactics over arbitrary standards of correct or incorrect ways of doing the liturgy, through an incapacity to distinguish the essential from the unessential. I for one could not possibly claim with any honesty that I preach the gospel with greater power by wearing a fourth-century alb and chasuble or a thirteenth-century surplice and hood than does my friend who wears a sixteenth-century black gown and bands or my sainted grandfather who wore a nineteenth-century frock coat and white tie.[1]

On the few occasions when I myself have dressed in the early nineteenth-century riding kit of an English bishop to make an official appearance as a father-in-God, I have not really felt dressed for the part.

It is unnecessary for me to say much about this conservatism. One can see its very valuable side—the faith is not something to change with every passing fashion, and probably the conservatives have often prevented distortion and dissipation of the faith through their preference for the old. Conservatism in these matters is sometimes unpredictable. In South India, the first draft of the C.S.I. Liturgy was printed and circulated by the Synod Executive before the Liturgy Committee had even seen it. At that

[1] M. H. Shepherd, "Liturgy and Mission", Article in *Liturgy is Mission*, ed. F. S. Cellier, 1964, p. 41.

stage it was the work of one man, and had not yet gone the rounds for criticism and comment. This first draft was taken up by the predominantly ex-Methodist Diocese of Medak and used at their Diocesan Council, with much misgiving on the part of most delegates. But they liked it so much that they then obstructed further revision, clinging to the first draft and opposing every good idea which was suggested by experts all over the world. Conservatism does not usually manifest itself so promptly, but once a decision has been made to change, people usually adapt themselves fairly quickly to the change. I hope that may be a comfort to those engaged in revision in the Churches.

There are at least three factors which ought to force the Church to re-examine its liturgy at the present time. The first is the evangelistic motive and purpose of the redeemed community. The majority of people in Europe are no longer practising members of the Christian community. The proportion of people in America who are members of a Church is higher than in Europe, but I imagine few American churchmen are wholly satisfied with the position. The Church throughout the old Christian lands has to wake to its evangelistic responsibilities which are as great as those of the Churches in Asia and Africa. It is in this evangelistic situation that we become more acutely aware of the inadequacies of our theology and of the irrelevance of much of our worship to Christian witness and service in the everyday conditions of our modern world. There is a spurious religiosity and aestheticism which deceives people. I was told of a church in the United States furnished with all the trappings of nineteenth-century Roman Catholicism, Stations of the Cross, statues, a tabernacle on the altar, the lot. A friend of mine was astonished to find this church belonged to one of the Protestant denominations and asked why they had decorated it in this manner. He was told that some people liked it that way. The stone altar was apparently only used to receive the alms; Holy Communion was celebrated at a Communion table in a less conspicuous place. Our own Church is sometimes guilty of equally meaningless antiquarianism in its

28

buildings and furniture. This kind of thing seems to me nonsense, and we are becoming progressively uneasy about many of the things we have taken for granted for many years. No matter how dear the cult and its language may be to us by a lifetime of associations, yet the Church must re-examine it drastically in the light of the evangelistic call. Liturgy which conveys God's word to men in a readily comprehensible way, and which makes it easy for men to share in response to that word, is a powerful evangelistic agent, both for those inside the fellowship but not as yet wholly committed, and for those outside who may come to church for some special occasion.

I do not know if I ought to make it clear that I am thinking of liturgy as the regular activity of the people of God; I am not speaking here of special evangelistic efforts, or worship popularized in one way or another as a special event. Quite apart from any special stunts, the regular continuing worship of the Church is a most consistent witness to the unseen God, if that worship is seen to mean a great deal to the worshippers. What I have in mind is the evangelistic motive which is forcing the Roman Catholic Church to re-examine everywhere the use of the vernacular in divine worship; I am not here thinking of the bold experiments of Fr Robert de Nobili in South India in the early seventeenth century, for example.

The second movement of our time which is forcing Christians to a reconsideration of liturgy and to reform is the movement towards Christian unity. The C.S.I. Liturgy was born in such a situation. When the Churches in South India united, their express intention was that worship should go on as before, but the fact of unity made it impossible to be content with denominational liturgies, and a new service, which would incorporate the inheritance of the various traditions, was called for. Similarly the *rapprochement* of Lutheran Churches in America has produced the new *Service Book and Hymnal*, which is an impressive and worthy achievement. A common liturgy is seen to be a very powerful instrument of unity, and in East Africa a common

29

liturgy for Holy Communion is now being prepared, even before the Churches approach the stage of negotiating for a united Church.

The third factor which has made re-examination of the liturgy imperative is the fresh knowledge brought to us by biblical theology in the last three decades. Just as the rediscovery of the Greek Testament was one of the most powerful factors which led to the Reformation, so the new understanding of liturgical origins and the insights of biblical theology in our own time also force us to consider again the way we express and do things in relation to God. The Liturgical Movement, which is influencing the Churches of the West, both Catholic and Reformed, very greatly, is inseparably connected with renewed study of the Bible, and has also led those engaged in it to ecumenical concern. In England the movement was brought to the notice of the clergy and informed laity by the publication of *Liturgy and Society* by Fr Gabriel Hebert, who was essentially a New Testament scholar. I have a personal interest in that book, for in 1933, one wet and cold afternoon I walked on Hampstead Heath with Fr Hebert. He had just finished his book, but had not fixed the title. He expounded the message of the book with great enthusiasm and by the time our walk was over had decided finally what it would be called. That book woke the Church of England up to the necessity for liturgical renewal and to the fact that the cult must be an integral part of the corporate Christian life of the Church in any place. It cannot be a private devotional exercise for the pious few without losing its nature as the response of the community in thanksgiving and dedication to the ongoing proclamation in word and life of the unchanging grace of God.

There is no time now to describe the Liturgical Movement, and little need when you have so many able and brilliant scholars in this country who have written many books and enlightened us all on this subject. The Liturgical Movement is one of the great means which the Holy Spirit is using to bring renewal to the Church and to promote its unity. It has made us all uneasy with our present liturgical practice and it is showing lines on which reform must come if our liturgy, no less than our life and our thought, is to be relevant to the age in which we live.

At the end of this lecture I wonder whether I have at all answered my question. Can the Christian liturgy be relevant to the contemporary world? The question is badly posed. Christian liturgy cannot be relevant to a world that does not believe, but it must be relevant to that world *for the Christians*. It must enable them to know what God is saying in their situation; it must also enable them to respond, as men and women of this age, not as trying to make themselves people of the Middle Ages or the Reformation. We are called to be the Body of Christ, the instrument of his saving love and life, now, in the milieu of our own work and contemporary situation, and for that service and witness God wishes to inspire and equip us through a liturgy relevant to our needs.

3

Christian Unity and Liturgy

In this lecture I want to speak about various controversial matters which concern the way we worship and which have long divided the Churches but on which there now seems to be a growing consensus and agreement. I should perhaps preface my remarks by saying that the average Christian in Great Britain, India, and Africa is hesitant about approaches to wider union precisely because he fears a united Church would demand uniformity of rite and ceremony. In the first days of the Christian Church there seems to have been no such uniformity. Uniformity was largely a product of the State's attempt to use established Christianity and its liturgy as a means of national integration and solidarity. This appears in Constantine's desire to use the unity of the Church to strengthen the unity of the Empire. It is seen most vividly in England after the Restoration of the Monarchy in 1660, and the Acts of Parliament which imposed penalties on any Englishman who did not worship according to the Order of the Book of Common Prayer, and who failed to take Holy Communion.

The unity of the Church certainly does not demand uniformity of worship. I think that most schemes for Church Union have followed the lead of the Church of South India. The uniting Churches bound themselves to use bread and wine and the Lord's words of institution in celebrating the Lord's Supper and to use water in the Name of the Trinity at Baptism. A number of elements in a full Communion Service were suggested to them, but there was no attempt at the beginning or now to force any kind of uniformity of worship. The Asian Commission which studied this subject in preparation for Montreal, put the matter rather nicely when they said: "Unity without uniformity, freedom without heresy, and indigenization without syncretism, should be the marks of liturgical reform."

I have already mentioned the fact that the movement towards Church unity is one of the important stimuli to liturgical revision in our situation. I wish now to pick out four matters on which there is a growing consensus in the Churches, and to illustrate this agreement from three sources, the Lambeth Conference of 1958, the Fourth World Conference on Faith and Order at Montreal in July 1963, and the Vatican Ecumenical Council of the last months of 1963.

THE CORPORATENESS OF WORSHIP

It is a commonplace observation that in Europe and America our society grows more and more fragmented, and the working population moves about the country, rarely being settled long in one place. The idea of the Church as the nation on its religious side, which still seems to the African common sense, has died in England, even though the Establishment of the Church of England and the parochial system both depend upon it. In America such an idea has always been repudiated, even though it was formative of certain States at the time of their founding.

But this fragmentation and individualization of society is an entirely modern phenomenon, as far as I know. In the Old Testament in most places, the whole nation, Israel, is God's child. It is with the whole people God deals, with them he made his covenant. All Israel was in the patriarchs and prophets with whom he dealt. The Israelite at worship does not consider himself an individual, he is God's because he is of Israel, because he belongs to the nation. In some way too the other nations of the world are related to God, and so is every created thing. The ultimate hope is the restoration of all creation to harmony, along with the glorification of Israel.

The unity of all life and the interdependence of all created things is a familiar part of what John Taylor calls the Primal

Vision.[1] It is found too in Indian thought. I remember a heated discussion with a Brahmin in a third-class compartment on an Indian railway, who maintained that I and a mango tree we saw out of the window were one. I denied the identity.

In the African context, and in the light of Old Testament teaching, and of St Paul on the Body of Christ, we ought to examine closely the corporateness of our worship, and the sense of interdependence shown in it—interdependence within the worshipping congregation itself, with the greater Church in all the world, with the Church triumphant in heaven, and with the created universe.

The only indigenous form of worship I know in Africa is the fellowship meeting of the Revival groups. These are informal meetings, but nevertheless a definite pattern has been evolved. There is a leader whose management of the group is unquestioned, but every member may speak if he is moved to do so and if he is, so to speak, allowed by the Chair. Testimonies of victory over sin or fear given by Christ are greeted with spontaneous singing of a hymn chorus, *Tukutendereza* (We praise thee), which has become not only a kind of theme song of the movement, but the equivalent of the more ancient Glory be to the Father, and to the Son, and to the Holy Spirit! If the community does not feel the testimony is genuine, there is a horrid little silence until someone else jumps up to speak. A fellowship meeting of this kind, with Bible study and an opportunity for testimony and expressions of praise and penitence, must be very like the Christian meeting referred to by St Paul in 1 Corinthians. It is essentially a corporate act.

So, too, is the celebration of the Eucharist in one of the ancient so-called Syrian Churches of South India. The whole parish attends the Eucharist, for there is only one service on a Sunday. The church buildings are always quite full at every Sunday Kurbana, or Eucharist, with a crowd of late-comers packing the doors and windows, if these are low enough. Through the whole course of the service the people are busy, chanting or bowing or

[1] J. V. Taylor, *The Primal Vision*, S.C.M. Press, 1963.

crossing themselves. Laymen and men in minor orders take their part in the service and at the moment of consecration the noise is almost deafening, as the people burst into a united chant, bombs are fired off outside the church and handbells and the church bell are vigorously rung. This is not all; the Peace is exchanged, a kind of ceremonial handshake, and all file past the bishop or priest at the end of the service to kiss his hand-cross. It is an immensely corporate occasion, with every member of the body taking an active part in the worship. There is little individual devotion about it from beginning to end, and little detailed comprehension—the prayers, until recently, being mostly in an unknown tongue.

The development of worship since the Middle Ages in Europe is in striking contrast. Low Mass in the Roman rite was said inaudibly and in a language people did not understand. The priest might refer to it as "my Mass". The people occupied their time with private prayers or the rosary, only attempting to join in the priest's action when the bell rang to recall them to their duties. In the Reformed tradition in many churches the people have hardly any part to play except singing the hymns and psalms and contributing to the collection. You must be familiar here with those devout Anglicans who much prefer an early morning Celebration on Sundays to a later congregational Eucharist, on the ground that there are fewer people at the early service and it is much quieter.

Nearly all the Churches are now feeling their way to a more truly corporate worship. The Report of Section IV of Montreal on Worship and the Oneness of Christ's Church recommends to all the Churches that they should consider seriously the more active participation of the laity in the liturgy and the reception of Communion by the whole assembled congregation as the normal practice whenever the Eucharist is celebrated.

The Montreal Report expresses this principle as follows:

The act of worship is the act of the whole congregation within which ministers and people exercise their spiritual gifts and offices (1 Cor. 12.7; 14.12; 1 Pet. 4.10,11). The leader of a service, therefore, is not a privileged man before God, but participates in the worship of the whole congregation as the one through whom some special parts of the spiritual ministry are performed. The congregation itself, on the other hand, participates in ministry, in particular by listening to the word of God, receiving the Holy Communion, praying, confessing, praising, and dedicating itself to the glory of God and the service of men. Thus the building up of the New Temple, the Church, takes place in and through the Holy Spirit.[1]

The Vatican Council has much to say on this:

Mother Church earnestly desires that all the faithful should be led to that full, conscious, and active participation in liturgical celebrations which is demanded by the very nature of the liturgy. Such participation by the Christian people as "a chosen race, a royal priesthood, a holy nation, a redeemed people" (1 Pet. 2.9; cf. 2.4,5), is their right and duty by reason of their baptism.

In the restoration and promotion of the sacred liturgy, this full and active participation by all the people is the aim to be considered before all else; for it is the primary and indispensable source from which the faithful are to derive the true Christian spirit; and therefore pastors of souls must zealously strive to achieve it, by means of the necessary instruction, in all their pastoral work.

Yet it would be futile to entertain any hopes of realizing this unless the pastors themselves, in the first place, become thoroughly imbued with the spirit and power of the liturgy, and undertake to give instruction about it. A prime need, therefore, is that attention be directed, first of all, to the liturgical instruction of the clergy.[2]

And again:

The Church, therefore, earnestly desires that Christ's faithful, when present at this mystery of faith, should not be there as strangers or silent spectators; on the contrary, through a good understanding of the rites and prayers they should take part in the sacred action conscious of what they are doing, with

<hr />

[1] *Report*, p. 22, 8.   [2] *Constitution*, 14.

devotion and full collaboration. They should be instructed by God's word and be nourished at the table of the Lord's body; they should give thanks to God; by offering the immaculate victim, not only through the hands of the priest, but also with him, they should learn also to offer themselves; through Christ the Mediator, they should be drawn day by day into ever more perfect union with God and with each other, so that finally God may be all in all.[1]

The Episcopal Conferences in each territory are to be responsible for deciding (subject to Rome's approval) how much of the Mass is to be in the vernacular, as a means of promoting this more truly corporate celebration.

The Lambeth Conference drew attention to features in the Books of Common Prayer which are effective in maintaining our doctrinal emphasis and witness. The first two points are relevant to our purpose:

1. Forms of worship in the vernacular.
2. Wholly *common* prayer; avoiding official private prayers of the celebrant while the people are otherwise engaged; avoiding prayer which cannot be heard by the congregation, and providing for the audible response of the congregation, and for communicants at every celebration.[2]

THE USE OF THE SCRIPTURES IN WORSHIP

The first part of the eucharistic liturgy has always been the reading and sometimes the preaching of God's Word. In the Syrian Church of South India very long readings from the Old Testament preface the Eucharist on great feasts. Nowadays these lessons are often read in the vernacular, but for centuries they were read in Syriac, which no one understood, though originally they had been translated into that language precisely because it was the vernacular, intelligible to those in east Syria who first brought the Church to Travancore. Then conservatism operated. The Syrians as a race died out. The Christian community was wholly Indian,

[1] *Constitution*, 48.
[2] *Lambeth Report 1958* (hereafter called *Lambeth*), 2.80.

not knowing a word of Syriac, and yet the old custom went on. Theological education for deacons (who were sometimes ordained as very young boys) and for priests was almost wholly teaching to chant the Syriac texts. The Scriptures were read, but the purpose of reading was wholly stultified by the unknown tongue.

In Europe also the Scriptures were read, but in Latin, and broken up by all kinds of responds and anthems, and interspersed with non-scriptural material, so that their value as a proclamation of God's Word was small.

The Reformation was above all else, liturgically, a return to the Bible. The Scriptures were translated into the European vernaculars and the expository sermon became the chief feature of the Reformed services. Logically, the only really impressive feature of a Reformed church was the pulpit. The communion table, in reaction to Roman altars, was usually insignificant.

Perhaps only in the Lutheran Church of Sweden has there been a conscious attempt, ever since the Reformation, to give equal prominence to pulpit and altar, to word and sacrament. This is now becoming normal everywhere—it is a direct result of the Liturgical Movement. Even so, delegates to an Anglican conference at Cuernavaca in Mexico who were shown round the Roman Catholic Cathedral by the Bishop were somewhat surprised to find two aumbries—in one the Sacrament reserved, and in the other a Bible!

There is much in the Lambeth Report about the Bible in the Church, but there are so many quotations in this lecture I fear to tire you by quoting too much. Let me read only two sentences:

The Church must live by the Bible. More than that, it must know itself as the Church of the Bible, the people of God.[1]

The Montreal Section IV Report says:

Christian worship in the form of preaching is based upon the commandment of Jesus Christ and his promise that he himself will be present with the hearers, working in them by his word.

[1] *Lambeth*, 2.13.

38

In the whole of Christendom, concern about liturgy directly involves preaching based upon the Holy Scriptures. Accordingly the task of the preacher is to proclaim the prophetic and apostolic word, as set forth in the Scriptures of the Old and New Testaments, and to interpret this word of God's judgement and mercy in the contemporary situation.[1]

The Montreal Report shows some of the difficulties involved. It points out that the whole question of the Bible's authority is still a battleground in many, perhaps most, Asian Churches.

Clear and positive teaching about the Bible and its authority in the light of contemporary scholarship is an urgent necessity, if Scripture is to be central, and the living Word in Worship.[2]

I know of African Churches which have not yet received the Old Testament in their own language and where those who have built up the Church are a little afraid of their people getting it because to their literal minds it will seem to support polygamy, tribal war, and various other things which do not accord with the Christian ethic.

The Vatican Council has much to say on the place of the Scriptures in worship:

Sacred scripture is of the greatest importance in the celebration of the liturgy. For it is from scripture that lessons are read and explained in the homily, and psalms are sung; the prayers, collects, and liturgical songs are scriptural in their inspiration, and it is from the scriptures that actions and signs derive their meaning. Thus to achieve the restoration, progress and adaptation of the sacred liturgy, it is essential to promote that warm and living love for scripture to which the venerable tradition of both eastern and western rites gives testimony.[3]

And again:

That the intimate connection between words and rites may be apparent in the liturgy:

1. In sacred celebrations there is to be more reading from holy scripture, and it is to be more varied and suitable.

[1] *Section IV Report*, 108(c).   [2] *Report*, p. 34.   [3] *Constitution*, 24.

2. Because the sermon is part of the liturgical service, the best place for it is to be indicated even in the rubrics, as far as the nature of the rite will allow; the ministry of preaching is to be fulfilled with exactitude and fidelity. The sermon, moreover, should draw its content mainly from scriptural and liturgical sources, and its character should be that of a proclamation of God's wonderful works in the history of salvation, the mystery of Christ, ever made present and active within us, especially in the celebration of the liturgy.

3. Bible services should be encouraged, especially on the vigils of the more solemn feasts, on some weekdays in Advent and Lent, and on Sundays and feast days. They are particularly to be commended in places where no priest is available; when this is so, a deacon or some other person authorized by the Bishop should preside over the celebration.[1]

PRESENCE AND SACRIFICE

People who agree on essentials can be divided by an attempt to define them, and sometimes, in fighting about definitions, the essential itself becomes obscured. From primitive days it was certainly believed that our Lord was present at the Eucharist of his people and also that the Eucharist was very closely connected with Christ's sacrifice of himself. There was no definition *how* he was present. The East was clear his presence is a mystery.

But in 1215 Transubstantiation was defined and accepted by the Church in the West. From that time the definition had to be accepted by the faithful. Christ became present in the Eucharist at a certain moment, when the words of institution were said, by change of the substance of bread and wine into that of the Body and Blood of Christ. Genuflexion was ordered to the Sacred Victim of the Altar, priests were handed the sacred vessels at their ordination with commission to offer sacrifice for the living and the dead, the Sacrament was to be lifted up for adoration. Always men had treated the Holy Bread with reverence, but now the mechanics of the miracle had been exposed. Christ could now

[1] *Constitution*, 35.

be found with certainty localized, confined to the place where the Bread and Wine were placed. And Christ, in the Bread and Wine, could now be lifted up and offered by men as a sacrifice to the Father, for the sins of the living or the dead. So Masses were multiplied and countless altars set up.

The reformers found this doctrine and practice intolerable. Luther, sure of the Presence of the Lord in the Sacraments, tried to find some less dangerous philosophic way of defining the connection. He could not bear the thought of man doing anything to add to the "once-for-allness" of Christ's death and he repudiated all idea of repeating that all-sufficient sacrifice. Other reformers gave up any attempt to define the mystery. They said Christ was truly present, but in the heart of the believer, not in the Bread and Wine of the Sacrament. All repudiated any idea of sacrifice in the Eucharist. I well remember a strong letter from a Continental Reformed theologian about the beginning of the Eucharistic Prayer in the C.S.I. Liturgy. You will recognize the words: "Truly holy, truly blessed art thou, O heavenly Father, who of thy tender love towards mankind didst give thine only Son Jesus Christ to take our nature upon him and to suffer death upon the cross for our redemption; who made there, by his own oblation of himself once offered, a full, perfect, and sufficient sacrifice, oblation, and satisfaction, for the sins of the whole world." Designed by Cranmer to repudiate a repeated sacrifice of Christ in the Eucharist, and insisted on by the Methodist element in the C.S.I. as a safeguard against misunderstanding by Hindus, to the Swiss theologian the very mention of the word sacrifice in connection with the Sacrament, was anathema.

Yet I believe, but here I may be naïve, that we are now approaching agreement at this very storm centre of liturgical controversy.

First, let us consider the question of Presence. I think that now most theologians are concerned much more with time than matter. The essence of presence is relation and action between the person present and the person with whom he is present. We habitually speak of the presence of Christ with us, through the Holy Spirit, with sufficient scriptural authority. Christ is not in time, as we are in time, and so he can be with us always, even to the end of the ages. What he said in his incarnate life is true at every time and what he did for our salvation he did once for all; for ever. "Christ offered for all time one sacrifice for sins, and took his seat at the right hand of God."[1] This is surely the meaning of anamnesis, of his memorial. The one event of Calvary where Jesus Christ gave himself for us on the first Good Friday is present to us, not repeated, not even re-presented, but recalled, a present reality, in the same way as in the preaching of the Cross the sinner is offered a present salvation. It is also what we mean when we end our prayers "through Jesus Christ our Lord".

Here I quote from Bishop Aulen of the Church of Sweden, and I take this quotation from a suggestive article by A. M. Allchin in *Studia Liturgica*:

> If the sacrifice offered once for all is eternally valid and relevant, and if it is one with Christ who is himself the sacrifice, then the presence of Christ in the sacrament includes the effective presence of his sacrifice. It is not a question of recalling something which happened two thousand years ago on Golgotha. The past is here too the present, as the Lord himself makes the past and eternally valid sacrifice contemporaneous with us. As the Lord on that last evening of his life presented the sacrifice which was momentarily to be made, and which signified the last act in his total sacrificial activity, and as he included his disciples in his sacrifice and united them with it, so also he includes his present disciples in the sacrifice which is eternally valid and eternally effective, and makes them partakers of the blessings flowing from the sacrament. . . . The real presence and the sacrifice belong together. *This sacrifice is present because the living Lord is present. But the living Lord cannot be present without actualizing his sacrifice.*[2]

The article from which I have quoted shows how other Lutheran writers, Reformed, and Roman Catholics, seem to approach this

[1] Heb. 10.12.
[2] G. Aulen, *Eucharist and Sacrifice*, 1958, pp. 192–3, quoted by A. M. Allchin in "The Eucharistic Offering", in *Studia Liturgica* 1.2. p. 106.

problem in very much the same way. The old controversy about "substance" seems dead.

Lambeth had this to say about it:

The sacrifice of Christ as the offering of willing obedience included not only his death on the Cross but all that contributed to it, of which it was the culmination. The finished work of Calvary is consummated in the resurrection and ascension.

This sacrifice is once and for all, but though it cannot be repeated, it is not merely a past fact; it is not only an event in history, but the revelation of eternal truth. He is the Lamb slain from the foundation of the world, now seated at the right hand of God after the power of an endless life. The fact revealed in time past has to be continually translated into the present by the operation of the Spirit. "He will take what is mine and declare it to you" (John 16.14).[1]

Montreal declares:

Through Christian worship in all its manifold forms the congregations in every age make a proclamation and celebrate a memorial (*anamnesis*) of the mighty acts of God in history, in order that the world may share in the love of God, the love by which he created the world, gave his Son for its salvation, and will in the end bring it to perfection. When those saving acts of God are proclaimed (in preaching) and commemorated (in the Eucharist) and confessed (in the prayers, confessions and thanksgivings of the community and of the individual), they are certainly not a "dead" past which we can only "recall" like any other historical events. They are of course real historical events. They *took place* once upon a time, and thus they have to be mentioned in the past tense. But when they took place they were events of universal importance, since they were God's mighty acts which he performed for the salvation of all mankind. Therefore they are always and everywhere present, where God, the almighty and merciful Creator of all things, decides to reveal himself to men in his only-begotten Son through his Holy Spirit. This abiding presence of God's revelatory acts in history, made contemporary through the Holy Spirit, is a presence *sui generis* which cannot be adequately expressed by means of any philosophical ontology. We must realize that we

[1] *Lambeth*, 2.84.

43

speak of a "mystery", when we speak of the presence of God's mighty acts in Christian worship.[1]

Very closely related to the converging views on the nature of Christ's Presence is the doctrine of Eucharistic Sacrifice. The argument of Lambeth was as follows:

In our baptism we were united with him by the likeness of his death (Rom. 6.5) and in the Eucharist we abide in him as we eat his Body and drink his Blood (John 6.56). So we come to the Father in and through Jesus our great High Priest. We have nothing to offer that we have not first received, but we offer our praise and thanksgiving for Christ's sacrifice for us and so present it again, and ourselves in him, before the Father. We are partakers of the sacrifice of Christ (1 Cor. 10.16), and this is shown forth by our sacrifice of praise to God continually through Christ (Heb. 13.15), and by our life of service and suffering for his sake in the world (Phil. 3.9,10). We ourselves, incorporate in the mystical body of Christ, are the sacrifice we offer. Christ with us offers us in himself to God. Accordingly the Committee endorses the words of Dr A. G. Hebert, s.s.m.: "The eucharistic Sacrifice, that storm-centre of controversy, is finding in our day a truly evangelical expression from the 'catholic' side, when it is insisted that the sacrificial action is not any sort of re-immolation of Christ, nor a sacrifice additional to his one Sacrifice, but a participation in it. The true celebrant, is Christ the High-Priest, and the Christian people are assembled as members of his Body to present before God his Sacrifice, and to be themselves offered up in Sacrifice through their union with him." This, however, involves a repudiation of certain medieval developments, notably the habitual celebration of the Eucharist without the Communion of the people; or the notion that the offering of the Eucharist is the concern of the individual priest rather than of the assembled Church; and, above all, any idea that in the Eucharist we offer a sacrifice to propitiate God. We offer it only because he has offered the one Sacrifice, once for all, in which we need to participate.[2]

Christ is not sacrificed again, there is no question of pleading his sacrifice with the Father. As Fr Hebert says in another place:

[1] Report, pp. 11, 12.   [2] Lambeth, 2.84, 85.

But can it be right to plead with God to accept the one sacrifice of his Son which he has once for all accepted when he raised him from the dead?[1]

We are taken into Christ's sacrifice and he offers himself in us and we in him to do the Father's will.

The holy, redeemed city itself, that is the congregation and society of the saints, is offered as a universal sacrifice to God through the high priest, who offered himself in suffering for us in the form of a servant, that we might be the body of so great a Head. . . . This is the sacrifice of Christians "the many are one body in Christ" which also the Church celebrates in the sacrament of the altar, familiar to the faithful, where it is shown to her that in this thing which she offers she herself is offered.[2]

I started this section by pointing out how the attempt to define God's action in the Eucharist eventually led to the disruption of the western Church. I do not think this doctrine can be defined, but I think that the Eucharist can properly be called a sacrifice, and all the congregation taught to offer themselves to God in it, through Christ and in the power of the Holy Spirit. And the sacrifice has then to be carried over to the places where we work and live, and offered daily, the sacrifice of obedience, of service, and of praise.

The Ecumenical Council does not make any fresh dogmatic statement on the matter of the eucharistic sacrifice. Sections 47 and 48 read as follows:

At the Last Supper, on the night when he was betrayed, our Saviour instituted the eucharistic sacrifice of his body and blood. He did this in order to perpetuate the sacrifice of the Cross throughout the centuries until he should come again, and so to entrust to his beloved spouse, the Church, a memorial of his death and resurrection: a sacrament of love, a sign of unity, a bond of charity, a paschal banquet in which Christ is eaten, the mind is filled with grace, and a pledge of future glory

[1] A. G. Hebert, *Apostle and Bishop*, 1963, p. 119.
[2] St Augustine, *The City of God*, ch. 10, sect. 6, quoted in Ramsey, *The Gospel and the Catholic Church*, p. 118. See also the quotations from St Augustine on p. 61.

is given to us. The Church, therefore, earnestly desires that Christ's faithful, when present at this mystery of faith, should not be there as strangers or silent spectators; on the contrary, through a good understanding of the rites and prayers they should take part in the sacred action conscious of what they are doing, with devotion and full collaboration. They should be instructed by God's word and be nourished at the table of the Lord's body; they should give thanks to God; by offering the immaculate victim, not only through the hands of the priest, but also with him, they should learn also to offer themselves; through Christ the Mediator, they should be drawn day by day into ever more perfect union with God and with each other, so that finally God may be all in all.[1]

It is clear, however, that the problem of reconciliation with the Roman Catholic Church on this doctrine remains. Hans Kung says:

Many very difficult theological questions concerning the doctrine of the Eucharist emerge in this connection. The theology of the Counter-Reformation was in many ways biassed and of a very dubious nature, especially where its teaching on the Eucharist was concerned. For example, the commemorative aspect of the Eucharist and its character as a feast, both of which were still in prominence in the Middle Ages, were neglected, whereas its sacrificial aspect was subjected to over-emphasis. Now, it is the concept of the sacrifice and the way in which it should be presented and brought home to the people which pose numerous questions which have still to be resolved. In any renewal of the Canon, the original proportions of the eucharistic prayer and its earliest perspectives would have to be taken carefully into account in the light of Holy Scripture.[2]

NOTE ON THIS SECTION

After delivering these lectures I have come across several rather astringent criticisms of the Lambeth statement written from an Evangelical point of view. John H. Rodgers says:

[1] *Constitution*, 47, 48.
[2] Hans Kung, *The Living Church*, 1963, pp. 187, 188.

We must say that the doctrine of the "Eucharistic Sacrifice" is no bridge at all but a re-expression of the same piety which took offence at the fullness of grace at the Reformation. It fails to see the truth that worship is fundamentally God's gift to man, before it can be man's response to God: it is a piety which still seeks to give along with Christ instead of receiving all from Christ and then, in response, in new freedom, to give all in gratitude.[1]

That is finely said. But we *are* called to follow Christ, to commit ourselves to him, and we feel that our choice is free. It must be *our* decision. Yet, when we do respond, we know it has been possible only in the power of the Holy Spirit, it is not of ourselves. Corporate commitment to God, in Christ, in the power of the Spirit, made possible only through Christ's one sacrifice for us, is the essence of the eucharistic sacrifice. I cannot see that is Pelagian or that it bears any resemblance to the medieval doctrine rejected at the Reformation.

CONSECRATION

Not all Anglicans realize how sold we are as a Church to the traditional western view of consecration. In the new African Liturgy there are no manual acts when the words of institution are recited in the course of the eucharistic prayer. An Evangelical bishop, on seeing the draft of that liturgy, wrote in horror that he could find no consecration. It is the western view, underlined in the 1662 provision for consecrating further bread or wine, that consecration is effected by using the words of institution of the Lord. Perhaps this view developed strongly as a defence against eastern criticism that the Roman rite had no epiclesis, for in the East from the time of Cyril of Jerusalem[2] there has been great stress on the necessity of an epiclesis on the bread and wine. This was considered to be the moment when the Holy Spirit changed the bread and wine into the Body and Blood of the Lord.

[1] *The Seminary Journal*, July 1964, Alexandria, Virginia, p. 19.
[2] *Mystagogical Catechesis*, V.5.

It is now, however, generally accepted that the earlier form of the epiclesis was an invocation of the Holy Spirit not upon the bread and wine but upon the worshippers, to enable them to fulfil their ministry. Hippolytus asks "that the Holy Spirit may be sent upon this offering of thy Holy Church: bringing her together in unity do thou bestow on all thy saints who receive it the fullness of the Holy Spirit to confirm our faith in truth".

Behind this division between East and West on the use of words of institution or an epiclesis of the Holy Spirit there seems to have been something much simpler. In the first days the Church did what the Lord himself had done; he gave thanks to God over the bread and wine, and it seems now to be established that for a Jew to give thanks to God over something is to bless it. So Justin speaks of the bishop giving thanks according to his ability. I believe that this understanding is becoming more and more accepted in Churches all over the world. Consecration is not our act, it is the act of the Great High Priest in our midst who is the Celebrant. He is in us as we give thanks to the Father, and so the bread and wine lying on the table placed there by us for God to use, although indeed they have come from him, become set apart by this thanksgiving, and he uses them to feed us with his life, his body and blood. The emphasis is not on the nature of his presence in relation to the bread and wine, but on him who takes them, breaks them, and gives them, and in doing so gives himself.

Here I quote Lambeth once more:

> We desire to draw attention to a conception of consecration which is scriptural and primitive and goes behind subsequent controversies with respect to the moment and formula of consecration. This is associated with the Jewish origin and meaning of *eucharistia* and may be called consecration through thanksgiving. "To bless anything and to pronounce a thanksgiving over it are not two actions but one." "Everything created by God is good, and nothing is to be rejected if it is received with thanksgiving; for then it is consecrated by the word of God and prayer."[1]

[1] 1 Tim. 4.4,5.

Thanksgiving unveils the glory and generosity of the Creator and the original meaning and purpose of creation. It releases man's response to what has been done for him in redemption and sets free the love implanted in him.

"The Word of God accepted by the People of God and coming back to God from the lips of those giving thanks, actually sanctifies the creatures over which it is pronounced."[1]

The last sentence is a quotation from the French Oratorian, Père Louis Bouyer, from his splendid book *Life and Liturgy*. This indicates that Rome too is now moving towards this new but old idea.

[1] *Lambeth*, 2.85.

4

Two Experimental Liturgies

The agreements I have demonstrated have already begun to influence almost every attempt now being made to make the Church's liturgical worship more relevant and more adequate for the Christians of to-day. The Vatican Council laid down certain general norms for liturgical reform. No. 25 reads: "The Liturgical books are to be revised as soon as possible; experts are to be employed on the task, and bishops are to be consulted, from various parts of the world."

I have already mentioned the very stimulating rôle of discussions and negotiations towards the realization of the unity of the Church in this matter of liturgical renewal. New liturgies are constantly being considered and prepared, and those I have seen confirm that the measure of agreement I have mentioned in my previous lecture is a fact and not to be dismissed as wishful thinking. I want now to describe the experimental eucharistic liturgy called A Liturgy for Africa, with side-glances at its parent, the C.S.I. Liturgy, and to preface this by reminding you of the points Lambeth 1958 said ought to be remembered in liturgical reform. These can be summarized as follows:

1. A Lesson from the Old Testament might be included in the Ministry of the Word at the principal Eucharist on Sundays.
2. Psalmody could be supplied between the readings.
3. The Sermon should follow the readings, before the Nicene Creed.
4. The Preparation for the Ministry of the Word should include *Gloria in excelsis* or *Te Deum*.
5. The People's Prayers should be restored by prayer in a litany form, or by breaking up the Prayer for the Church into a kind of litany.

6. The Offertory, with which the people should be definitely associated, should be more closely connected with the Prayer of Consecration.
7. The events for which thanksgiving is made in the Consecration Prayer are not to be confined to Calvary but are to include thanksgiving for all "the principal mighty works of God", especially the resurrection and ascension of our Lord, and his return in glory.

All these suggestions had been, in fact, already carried out in the *Order for the Lord's Supper or Holy Eucharist*, of the Church of South India, first published in 1950 and not substantially changed since. As I said before, there had been no intention in the C.S.I. to draw up a new Liturgy for Holy Communion, at least for some years. But the demand for a new Order of Service was made almost immediately after the Inauguration of Union in September 1947. At that Inauguration Service the Book of Common Prayer rite was used, but by the end of the year dioceses which brought together several traditions were clamouring for a new rite which would remind them not of past differences but of present unity. Scholars and churchmen of many traditions commented on our drafts, and since Synod accepted the final draft the Liturgy has been used not only in South India, but often at ecumenical gatherings all over the world. For example, the Committee of the All-Africa Conference of Churches asked that the Thanksgiving Service for the inauguration of that body should be a service of Holy Communion, which should follow the C.S.I. rite.

One of the most heartening comments on the C.S.I. Liturgy came from Père Louis Bouyer, who said:

Now there is no doubt whatever that, while it skilfully incorporates quite unexceptionable Protestant customs, still, from the point of view of even a conservative Catholic (or Orthodox) liturgist, this eucharistic liturgy seems much more satisfactory than any liturgy that emanated from the Reformation. Unquestionably, it is much superior to the Prayer Book of the

Church of England both on account of its traditional character and its theological soundness.[1]

And again:

Supposing that validly ordained ministers used it, it seems difficult to deny that they would validly consecrate the eucharist. In any case, the Catholic Church would certainly have much less difficulty in letting these Indian Christians continue to use such a liturgy, if ever they came to her, than she would, under the same conditions, in letting any Protestant or Anglican community continue to use their rites and formularies to which they are accustomed.[2]

But the comment I like most came from a small boy leaving the Cathedral in Bangalore with his mother after attending the Liturgy: "Mummy, wasn't that a lovely service. We all joined in all the time."

One important fact, however, has to be remembered. The uniting Churches in South India were all evangelical in their theology. This fact made it easier for agreement to be reached on a liturgy than would have been the case had very differing theological traditions been represented. In a way, the problem facing the five Anglican provinces in Africa is more difficult, as every shade of ecclesiastical complexion within the Anglican family of Churches is represented, from the strong Protestant emphasis of Sydney, Australia, and the C.M.S., to the Anglo-Catholic tradition of the Universities' Mission to Central Africa or the Church of the Province of South Africa.

The first official draft of the Liturgy was drawn up by representatives of all the provinces at a meeting in Kampala in April 1963; it was then revised by the Provincial Liturgical Commissions and submitted to the Liturgical Consultation of all the Anglican Churches, held in Toronto immediately after the Congress last August. The archbishops desired that no further revision should take place until after a period of experimental use, but

[1] R. P. Louis Bouyer in *Theology*, LIX.427, January 1956, p. 4.
[2] Ibid., pp. 6, 7.

they had no authority to decide this matter, and some provinces insisted that further revision should take place before authorizing the Liturgy for use in their provinces. This has now been done, and the Liturgy printed with these lectures has various degrees of authorization for use within the provinces of South Africa, Central Africa, East Africa, and Uganda. It is hoped that West Africa, who were involved in the early stages of preparation in this Liturgy, will also make use of it in the liturgical work which will probably start in connection with the Nigeria and Ghana Church Union schemes. This African Liturgy was asked for in an attempt to create greater unity in provinces where different rites were used, sometimes different rites by different races. The success or failure of this Liturgy will not be apparent for some years, until it has had fairly wide use.

A Liturgy for Africa starts with an Introduction which makes two points important for our present purpose. First, the Liturgy is designed to become the chief Sunday service of every congregation—whether a priest is present or not. This reflects the state of the African Churches. In most areas every priest is responsible for a number of congregations. When I arrived in my own diocese I found one priest, with no ordained assistant, responsible for ninety congregations, but I suppose the average with us may be about fifteen. The first three parts of the new Liturgy—the Preparation, the Service of the Word of God, and the Intercession —may be conducted by a deacon or an authorized layman, thus ensuring that all the faithful join in common hearing of the Word of God and in intercession. The second point is that all God's people should participate actively in this act of worship. The people join in at every stage, even during the Eucharistic Prayer proper, the Great Thanksgiving, and the priest may be assisted by deacons and laymen (and women too) authorized by the priest himself.

The Directions, or general rubrics, need not occupy us long. It is intended that the first three parts of the service shall be conducted from whatever place is customary for non-eucharistic services. Only after that does the priest go to the Lord's Table. He may stand in the position customary in that congregation, but it is recommended he stands at the back of the Table, facing the people. Those who have used this position are united, I think, in feeling it is by far the most convenient position for the celebrant. No directions are given for the posture of the worshippers, but this is left for local custom, as we found that in some parts, for example, Central Africa, everyone stood for the Canon, whereas in other parts anything other than kneeling would be thought almost blasphemous.

The directions about announcing the Lessons assume that the people will have brought their own Bibles with them to church, to follow the readings, and prescribe that in the shortened form of the service either the Old Testament Lesson *or* the Epistle may be omitted.

Contrary to our normal western custom, there are no proper Prefaces in the Liturgy, the collects, readings, hymns, and other proper prayers being considered sufficient to mark the season. The climax of the whole service, the Great Thanksgiving, is itself an extended Preface—though it is no longer something "said before", but the heart of the matter, an inseparable part of the fourfold action of the Eucharist on which the Service of the Lord's Supper in this Liturgy is structured.

THE PREPARATION

The contents of the Preparatory part of the service—preparatory, that is, to the hearing of the Word and the reception of the Sacrament, are a matter of considerable difference of opinion. Some people feel that all that is needed is a hymn of praise before we go straight to the hearing of God's Word. Others feel that a moment for penitence and realization of the awfulness of what we are to do must be provided in the liturgy itself, preferably at this point. In the C.S.I. Liturgy there is such an introduction; but a good deal of the penitential material has been removed to a separate Service of Preparation, to be held in the week before the Celebration of the Eucharist, either in church or in private houses. This would be ideal, if one could be confident that it would be carried out, and not remain just a pious rubrical wish! It may well be that what is needed is a simplification of the Preparation of the priest and his attendants which forms the first public part of the Roman Mass, and which includes a psalm of approach and a responsive confession, although in our case we should require an active part for the people. Some Anglican Churches do have a preparation of priest and servers before the altar before the Service of Holy Communion celebrated according to the Prayer Book, but this seems unnecessary and confused when there is a confession and absolution for all later in the Service.

In most Churches of our Communion of Africa and Asia, where the number of priests is quite inadequate for the Holy Communion to be celebrated every Sunday, Morning Prayer has been the normal weekly worship for most Christians. If the first three parts of this liturgy are used instead of Morning Prayer it is important that the canticles and psalms of the daily office should still be known and used by the people, and so in this service opportunity is given at various points for such use. For example, at the beginning of the Preparation, the *Venite* may be said or sung, or another hymn or psalm.

The first prayer (as in C.S.I.) is the so-called Collect for Purity— but really a supplication that God the Holy Spirit will enable us to worship. It is almost an epiclesis on the whole of what we are about to do.

The Preparation is mostly penitential. You will remember that Cranmer's first step in reform of the liturgy was to insert into the Mass what he called A Short Order of Communion, in the vernacular, immediately after the Canon. This was an exhortation, the confession, absolution, comfortable words, prayer of humble access, and words of administration of the Sacrament. Since then, the position of these communion devotions has been altered in various prayer books. It may be that the right place for confession is where it is now in the 1662 and American books, after the preaching and the intercession. The Reformed would certainly agree with that. But here we have put all this penitential material at the beginning of the service, as a preparation for hearing and receiving God's Word no less than receiving the Sacrament.

The Ten Commandments or the Lord's Summary of the Law are read at this point, as some people consulted felt strongly they could not be omitted. The Law comes before the Gospel. In South India we found the commandments here made the service start on too heavy and sombre a note, so they were transferred to a Devotional Service conducted either in church or in private houses during the week before the actual Eucharist Service. In Africa the Kyrie is permitted as an alternative to the commandments. After this, the short exhortation in the Prayer Book is said, with its language modified a little. Here, incidentally, is another little problem. When you use material taken from another source ought you to reproduce it in its original form, or is it in order to modify it to suit your purposes? In this Liturgy this is what we have done, but some do not agree with us. There is a related problem which perhaps I should mention. Anglican liturgies all over the world use many of the same elements—like the Lord's Prayer, the Creed, the *Gloria in excelsis*, and so forth—but we use different forms of the same thing. May we hope that one day an effort will be made to agree on a common form for such common elements? The exhortation ends on a new note—telling us to confess our sins that we may be reconciled anew to God and to one another, through Christ.

Three forms of confession are provided. The first is adapted from the C.S.I. form (whose immediate ancestry is in the Book of Common Order of the Church of Scotland). This is followed by gracious words of God as an absolution. The second is a responsive form, rather like the Priest and Servers' Confession before going to the altar at Mass, or like the Confession in the new Anglican Japanese rite. The minister (remember he may not be a priest) confesses his sins and the people absolve him. Then they confess and he absolves them. If a priest is present he adds another absolution. This form came in from very High Church sources; it rather intrigues me, as I had always been brought up to believe that no one but a priest ought to absolve. The third confession is very short, followed by a prayer of absolution said by the minister or by the absolution itself if a priest is present.

This Preparation finishes with the *Gloria in excelsis* as a hymn of praise for God's mercy and forgiveness in Christ. In C.S.I. the *Gloria* comes at the beginning of the service, immediately after the first prayer for the Holy Spirit.

THE SERVICE OF THE WORD OF GOD

This is the second part of the service. In Luganda the title is rather splendidly translated *Okugabula*, the word used of distributing good food at a feast. This section starts with the mutual greeting and the collect of the day. Some critics insisted that the collect was nothing to do with the readings and so should be the last prayer of the Preparation, but here we follow the South India use, even if it is of doubtful provenance, and we regard the collect as a prayer preparing us to hear God's word and connected in subject matter with the scriptural readings.

The readings pose another problem. C.S.I. has arranged a thematic series connected with its threefold division of the Church's year—Sundays before and after Christmas, Sundays before and after Easter, Sundays before and after Pentecost. Each Sunday has its own theme, either of the season, or, after Pentecost, concerned with the Christian life. For the sake of example, the nineteenth Sunday after Pentecost deals with the Family. The collect refers to Christ's earthly home at Nazareth and prays that the members of our families may be bound to each other by mutual love. The Old Testament Lesson is Proverbs 4.1-9 dealing with Father and Son, the Proper Psalm 127, "Unless the Lord build the house", the Epistle Ephesians 5.21—6.4 in which St Paul deals with Family Life, the Gospel Mark 10.1–16, our Lord on marriage and the value of children. The Lessons at the evening service are, in South India, connected with the Eucharistic Readings, in this particular case 2 Samuel 18.24–33, David and Absalom, and I Peter 3.1–9, another passage on husbands and wives. This is one way of dealing with the problem; the objection may be that it leaves much of the Bible unread and, by defining the theme of each Sunday, may seem to limit the exposition of God's Word.

Another possible way of arranging the lessons is to read in course. The Roman Catholic Church is working on eucharistic lessons arranged in a four-year course, to cover most of the Bible. But now this work will quite likely be taken from the Congregation of Rites, and the regional Bishops' Meetings may have a good deal of liturgical power given to them to decide such things. However, it seems plainly desirable for the same readings to be used over as wide an area of the Church as possible, both as a means to genuine unity in confrontation with God's Word and also for convenience in printing prayer books.

We have not yet grappled with this problem in Africa, but each province will make its own arrangements, probably by suggesting Old Testament lections and a Proper Psalm which seem congruous with the New Testament readings. There is an Old Testament lesson, followed by the Proper Psalm or the *Benedicite*. Then the Epistle. The Gradual may be either *Te Deum*, *Benedictus*, or a psalm or hymn. The Gospel is read and the Sermon follows immediately. The intention is clear. It is that the sermon shall be closely connected with the readings and be an exposition of God's Word—not a moral essay, or good advice based on a poem or a pop song. The sermon is itself sacramental—through it God speaks a contemporary word. We have a long way to go before this understanding characterizes every Anglican service.

The Sermon is followed by the Creed commonly called Nicene. This is intended to be used not just as a declaration of intellectual assent to the Christian symbol, still less as a statement against the heretics, but with full weight given to the preposition "in"—as an act of existential commitment and trust in the Triune God in our present contemporary situation.

THE INTERCESSION

Here is the People's Prayer, when the whole congregation joins in prayer for the Church and the world. In South India two litanies are provided. The first is the Anglican Prayer for the Church Militant, expanded and broken up into suffrages, with the people's response between. The second is based on intercessions in the Liturgy of St James and was first used at the Inauguration Service of C.S.I., with the response "Lord, have mercy". Or, instead of the Litany, "the presbyter offers intercession in his own words for the Church and the world".

In the African Liturgy we have put in a very simple litany indeed, so constructed that petition for almost anything may be inserted (and is permitted) without breaking the rhythm of the prayer, provided it is put in the simple form "For so-and-so, we pray to thee, O God", with the people's response "Hear us, good Lord". Besides the traditional biddings we have inserted petitions for teachers, all who influence others by word, our homes, all men and women in their daily work, the homeless and the unemployed, and all who are persecuted. But the rubric is very wide: "The Minister may use any, or all of the following petitions and add others at his discretion."

The permission to omit is designed especially to help those who cannot conscientiously pray the last simple petition: "For all who have departed this life, in thy faith and fear, we pray to thee, O God." I myself see nothing theologically objectionable in this, and I think it is important in Africa, where the ancestors are a real factor in most people's lives, but there is one province which has said it cannot use the Liturgy if this petition is retained. However, like all the other petitions, its use is optional.

From the Intercession, if a priest is present, we go straight on to the Service of the Lord's Supper, the fourth part of our service. But, as I have said, in most African congregations a priest is not usually present. So, in these cases a hymn is sung, and the gifts of the people are brought up and placed on the Lord's Table with the same words as in the Eucharist itself. The General Thanksgiving follows, said by all, so that even without the Sacrament the element of thanksgiving and eucharist comes into the worship, and is followed by the Lord's Prayer and "the Grace of our Lord Jesus Christ".

THE SERVICE OF THE LORD'S SUPPER

This starts immediately after the final collect of the Intercession. There is no break, but the priest comes from his place, kneels before the Table, and leads the people in a simplified form of the Prayer of Humble Access. Then a hymn may be sung and lay people prepare the gifts of the people (either already collected at the back of the church before the service starts or collected now) and the bread and wine, to bring to the Table.

The hymn over and the preparations complete, the priest, still in front of the Table, salutes the people with the greeting of Peace, as the Lord did on Easter night. Provision is made, where desired, for the priest to touch hands with those in the sanctuary and for them to come down to the congregation, who pass it from hand to hand with the greeting. You cannot do this if you are scattered in tiny groups over a large church—you must be together. The handshake and mutual greeting is a very important and significant part of life to most Africans. In the villages one must never pass anyone, even a stranger, without greeting. So once people are used to this ceremony it is likely to be meaningful. In South India the "kiss of peace" is also given by a touch of the hands and is derived directly from the Syrian Church who use it in all their services. Indeed, minor excommunication is shown by denying a man this sign of fellowship. It was the Methodist element in South India who welcomed this in that Liturgy. I see that Professor Watkins of Christian Theological Seminary has included it in his service "An Order of Holy Communion".[1]

I am sorry that this was shot down by Professor G. Edwin Osborn of the Disciples of Christ, who says: "I doubt that the 'peace' ritual, so meaningful to the Oriental as a symbol of brotherliness and akin to some of his native customs . . . could ever mean much other than a sentimental or silly gesture to the sanitary-conscious Occidental."[2]

Well, there you are. It looks as if the Peace will not get into a union liturgy in America. In the African Liturgy the outward action is optional, not compulsory. In any case the salutation is put here to remind the people of the doctrine of St Augustine I quoted in my third lecture. The sacrifice we offer is our unity in Christ, we offer ourselves in the bread and the wine.

> If then you are the body and members of Christ, your mystery is placed on the Lord's Table, you receive your mystery. To that which you are you answer Amen, and you assent by your answer. For you hear "The Body of Christ" and you reply Amen. Be then a member of Christ's body in order that the Amen may be true.
> There are *you* upon the table, there are *you* in the chalice.[3]

And our Lord said, "First be reconciled to your brother and then come and offer your gift".[4]

After the Peace, lay people bring the gifts and the bread and wine for Communion to the priest, who places them on the Lord's Table, saying words from David's prayer in 1 Chronicles 29.11, with the people's response from the same prayer. You will note that the eucharistic dialogue starts with the Peace, the priest and people doing everything together, in dependence on the Holy Spirit and interdependence in the Body of Christ. The first action of the Lord's Supper has taken place—he took bread, he took wine.

---

[1] *Encounter*, Vol. 24, No. 3, Summer 1963, pp. 303 ff.   [2] Ibid., p. 328.
[3] St Augustine, *Sermons* 72 and 272. Quoted D. Webster, *Local Church and World Mission*, p. 90.
[4] Matt. 5.24.

The *Sursum Corda* initiates the second action—the blessing of God, the thanksgiving to God. This Great Thanksgiving is, of course, addressed to God the Father. First, thanks are offered through Christ, through whom God has made and sustains the worlds, the world we know, the countless galaxies of which the astronomers tell us. We thank God for the harmony of all creation and the many material blessings we enjoy. Then we go on to thank him for our redemption in Christ, his incarnation, his death, his resurrection, and his ascension, and for his perpetual intercession for us. Again we thank God for the Holy Spirit and for the priesthood of the world the Christian people have in Jesus. Whether or not a similar phrase in Hippolytus, our first complete eucharistic prayer, was there because Hippolytus' rite was used at an ordination, I do not know. The conception as we have it seems entirely relevant to our Christian duty and responsibility in the world.

This thanksgiving is really the body of the prayer, it leads up to the *Sanctus*, said or sung by all.

A petition asking that the communicants may receive the Body and Blood of the Lord in the Sacrament leads to a recital of the words of the Lord over the bread and cup, though there are no manual acts at this point. The people again join in, with words going back at least fourteen centuries in the Syriac rites: "His death, O Father, we proclaim. His resurrection we confess. His coming we await. Glory to thee, O Lord."

The last section of the prayers offers our praise again to God for all he has done for us in Christ, and the praise is offered in connection with the particular Bread and Cup lying on the Table, which has now been taken by the Lord and will be used for his redemptive purpose. The celebrant may at this point take the Bread and Cup into his hands. The prayer ends with asking him for the Holy Spirit to fill us and make us truly one body in Christ. The Our Father follows immediately and completes the Great Thanksgiving.

There is silence then for a little, and then the priest breaks the

Bread, as the Lord did, to give to his disciples. Holy Communion follows at once—"He broke; he gave."

There is very little else to say. Any blessing in words would seem trivial compared with the supreme blessing of receiving our Lord in his Sacrament. So there is silent thanksgiving, perhaps Psalm 103 or another song, a brief prayer that we may be kept faithful, and we are dismissed: "Go forth in the name of the Lord." "Thanks be to God." "After they had sung a hymn, they went out." And so the people of God ought to go out, back in the world to service and witness, one body living by one Spirit.

I do not know what you will think of this service. Some people saw it in one seminary in the West of Canada and thought it not radical enough. This may be true, but then any liturgical order has to be relevant to the people for whom it was prepared, and we can never expect to see a world liturgy. An even truer criticism would be that the Liturgy has nothing specifically African in it. As a matter of fact, in my own province the one thing about the Liturgy that causes disquiet is its name—the Africans say a liturgy cannot be African, it must be universal. Yet as the Church in Africa loses its fears of its own rich heritage of thought and vision in its own not-understood and consciously forgotten but still active African past, and claims all that for Christ, one can hope that forms of worship will come spontaneously from that free and joyously serving Church. But it is not men, it is only the Holy Spirit, who can make liturgy relevant and create a relevant liturgy.

APPENDIX

A LITURGY FOR
AFRICA

INTRODUCTION

The Archbishops of the Anglican Communion in Africa met in April 1961 and asked that consultations should take place between the Provinces with a view to composing a new Liturgy for the Holy Communion. The Archbishops hoped that such a Liturgy might win wide acceptance and form a bond of unity between Anglicans all over the continent. This Liturgy, prepared in answer to that request, was drafted at a meeting in Kampala in April 1963 of representatives of the Provinces of South Africa, West Africa, Central Africa, East Africa, and Uganda, and has been amended in the light of criticisms made by the Provincial Liturgical Commissions, and by the Liturgical Consultation of the Anglican Communion held at Toronto in August 1963. It is expected that further revision will be undertaken only after some years of experimental use. The Liturgy is intended for such experimental use as the Bishop of the Diocese shall authorize subject to the regulation of the competent Body in each Province.

The Liturgy is intended to be used as the chief Sunday service of a congregation when a priest is present. Even when there is no priest available, the first three sections of the Liturgy, namely the Preparation, the Service of the Word of God, and the Intercession, may be used, so that the congregation, though unable to receive the Sacrament, may join with their brethren in a common worship.

Where it is felt that the pattern of Mattins and Evensong according to the Prayer Book should be maintained, celebrations of the Holy Communion which follow these Offices could properly be according to this Liturgy, starting with the Service of the Lord's Supper. In such a case it is suggested that the Intercession should be used in place of the prayers after the Third Collect at Morning or Evening Prayer. This avoids any necessity for the shortening of the Choir Office or the abbreviation of the Prayer Book Order of Holy Communion.

At this stage no attempt is made to deal with a suggested revision of the whole pattern of daily and Sunday worship, but it is recognized that in due course attention will have to be given to this and, in particular, a new table of psalms and readings will have to be provided for use on Sundays and Holy Days.

Asterisks in the text indicate those sections which may be omitted at the discretion of the minister. An order, thus shortened, may also be used at extra celebrations on Sunday, additional to the main Sunday celebrations of the congregation.

The Liturgy is designed to ensure the fullest possible active participation of all God's people in worship. The full Liturgy, including the Service of the Lord's Supper, requires the presence of the bishop or a priest. In this case he should be assisted by a deacon (whether a man in deacon's orders or a priest acting in that capacity) and men authorized by the parish priest. In the absence of a priest, deacons or authorized laymen may conduct the Preparation, the Service of the Word of God, and the Intercession, as already noted. They may not celebrate the Service of the Lord's Supper.

Throughout the Liturgy the word "minister" is used to denote the person conducting that part of the Liturgy.

Directions for the use of the Liturgy

Position of the Minister

It is recommended that the celebrant does not go to the Lord's Table until the beginning of the Service of the Lord's Supper and that he stand either behind the Table facing the people, or in the customary position.

The Preparation, the Service of the Word of God, and the Intercession may be conducted from the place where the prayers are accustomed to be said, and the Bible read.

The Congregation's Part

Those parts of the Liturgy to be said by the congregation are printed in heavier type.

Singing in the Service

The use of the words "say" or "said" in the rubrics of the Liturgy does not preclude the singing of suitable parts of the service.

The Posture of the Worshippers

Usually directions have not been given as customs vary greatly between the Provinces. It is recommended that each Province follows local custom in this matter.

The Lessons

If it is necessary to shorten the Service, *either* the Old Testament Lesson *or* the Epistle may be used, the other being omitted.

Reading the Lessons

The Old Testament Lesson and Epistle are introduced as follows:
    The Lesson (*or* Epistle) is written in such and such a Book (*or* the Epistle of . . . to the . . .), chapter . . ., beginning at verse . . .
After the reading the reader says:
    Here ends the Lesson (*or* the Epistle).
The Gospel thus:
    The Holy Gospel is written in that according to St . . ., chapter . . ., beginning at verse . . .
The reader does *not* say anything at the end of the reading.
    After announcing each lesson the reader may pause while the people find the text in their Bibles.

The Sermon

A Sermon is to be preached, but at extra Celebrations of Holy Communion on Sundays, and at weekday Celebrations, it may be omitted if necessary.

Announcements

Announcements may be made after the creed.

The Collection of Alms and Gifts

It is recommended that such arrangement for the collection of the alms of the people be made as shall avoid the interruption or undue lengthening of the action in the Service of the Lord's Supper. If some persons leave before the Lord's Supper, they should be given opportunity to make their offerings before they leave.

Proper Prefaces

No Proper Prefaces are prescribed for use with this Liturgy, the season being sufficiently marked by the collect, readings, hymns, and other proper prayers.

A LITURGY FOR AFRICA

The Preparation

At the entry of the Ministers the Venite, verses 1-7, is said, otherwise a hymn or psalm may be used.

The Minister says:

Let us pray.

Almighty God, unto whom all hearts are open, all desires known, and from whom no secrets are hid, cleanse the thoughts of our hearts by the inspiration of thy Holy Spirit, that we may perfectly love thee, and worthily magnify thy holy name, through Jesus Christ our Lord. **Amen.**

God spoke these words saying: I am the Lord your God; you shall have no other gods before me.
Lord, have mercy upon us, and incline our hearts to keep this Law.

You shall not make yourself a graven image, or any likeness of any thing that is in heaven above, or that is in the earth beneath, or that is in the water under the earth. You shall not bow down to them, or serve them.

or Our Lord Jesus Christ said: You shall love the Lord your God with all your heart, and with all your soul, and with all your strength, and with all your mind; and your neighbour as yourself.
Lord, have mercy upon us, and write these thy Laws in our hearts, we beseech thee.

or Lord, have mercy.
Christ, have mercy.
Lord, have mercy.

or

Lord, have mercy.
Lord, have mercy.
Lord, have mercy.
Christ, have mercy.
Christ, have mercy.
Christ, have mercy.
Lord, have mercy.
Lord, have mercy.
Lord, have mercy.

71

Lord, have mercy
upon us, and incline
our hearts to keep
this Law.

You shall not take
the name of the Lord
your God in vain.
Lord, have mercy
upon us, and incline
our hearts to keep
this Law.

Remember the
Sabbath day, to
keep it holy.
Lord, have mercy
upon us, and incline
our hearts to keep
this Law.

Honour your father
and your mother.
Lord, have mercy
upon us, and incline
our hearts to keep
this Law.

You shall not kill.
Lord, have mercy
upon us, and incline
our hearts to keep
this Law.

You shall not
commit adultery.
Lord, have mercy
upon us, and incline
our hearts to keep
this Law.

You shall not steal.
Lord, have mercy upon
us, and incline our

72

hearts to keep this Law.

You shall not bear false witness against your neighbour.
Lord, have mercy upon us, and incline our hearts to keep this Law.

You shall not covet.
Lord, have mercy upon us, and write these thy Laws in our hearts, we beseech thee.

*Then the Minister exhorts the people in these or like words:

You who truly and earnestly repent of your sins, and are in love and charity with your neighbours, and intend to lead the new life, following the commandments of God and walking from henceforth in his holy ways, make your humble confession to Almighty God, that you may be reconciled anew to him and to one another through our Lord Jesus Christ.

After a short silence the Minister and people say:

Heavenly Father, we confess that we have sinned against thee and our neighbour. We have walked in darkness rather than light; we have named the name of Christ, but have not followed him. Have mercy upon us, we beseech thee; for the sake of Jesus Christ forgive us all our sins;

or After a short silence the Minister says:

I confess to God Almighty, the Father, the Son, and the Holy Spirit, before the whole company of heaven and you all, that I have sinned exceedingly in thought, word, and deed, through my own grievous fault; wherefore I pray God to have mercy upon me and you to pray for me.

or After a short silence the Minister and people say:

We confess to God Almighty, the Father, the Son, and the Holy Spirit, before the whole company of heaven that we have sinned exceedingly in thought, word, and deed, through our own grievous fault: wherefore we pray God to have mercy upon us.

bring us to true repentance; cleanse our hearts and consciences by thy Holy Spirit: that we may receive power to forgive others and to serve thee in newness of life, to the glory of thy holy name. Amen.

Then the Minister says:

Hear the gracious word of God to all who truly turn to him in penitence and faith:

Come to me, all who labour and who are heavy-laden, and I will give you rest.

If anyone sins, we have an advocate with the Father, Jesus Christ the righteous; and he is the expiation for our sins, and not for ours only but also for the sins of the whole world.

If we confess our sins, he is faithful and just, and will forgive our sins and cleanse us from all unrighteousness.

And the people say:

Almighty God have mercy upon you, forgive you all your sins, and bring you to eternal life.

Then the people make confession:

We confess to God Almighty, the Father, the Son, and the Holy Spirit, before the whole company of heaven and you, that we have sinned exceedingly in thought, word, and deed, through our own grievous fault: wherefore we pray God to have mercy upon us and you to pray for us.

And the Minister says:

Almighty God have mercy upon you, forgive you all your sins, and bring you to eternal life.
Amen.

And the Minister says:

Almighty God have mercy upon us, forgive us all our sins, and preserve us in eternal life.
Amen.

If a Priest is present, he says:

The Almighty and Merciful Lord grant unto you pardon, absolution, and remission of all your sins. **Amen.**

Then all say:

Glory to God in the highest, and on earth peace among men in whom he is well pleased. We praise thee, we bless thee, we worship thee, we glorify thee, we give thanks to thee for thy great glory, O Lord God, heavenly King, God the Father Almighty.

O Lord, the only-begotten Son Jesus Christ, O Lord God, Lamb of God, Son of the Father, who takest away the sin of the world, have mercy upon us; thou who takest away the sin of the world, receive our prayer. Thou who sittest at the right hand of God the Father, have mercy upon us.

For thou only art holy, thou only art Lord, thou only art most high, O Jesus Christ, with the Holy Spirit, in the glory of God the Father. Amen.

The Service of the Word of God

The Lord be with you.
And with thy spirit.

Then the Minister says the Collect of the day and additional Collects if prescribed.

OLD TESTAMENT LESSON

After the Old Testament Lesson, one of the Proper Psalms or the Benedicite *is said.*

THE EPISTLE

After the Epistle, the Te Deum, *or in Advent and Lent the* Benedictus, *is said. Otherwise, a hymn or psalm may be used.*

THE HOLY GOSPEL

After the Gospel has been announced the people say:

Glory be to thee, O Lord.

Then the reading is ended the people say:

Praise be to thee, O Christ.

*THE CREED COMMONLY CALLED NICENE:

I believe in one God: the Father Almighty, Maker of heaven and earth, and of all things visible and invisible:

And in one Lord Jesus Christ, the only-begotten Son of God; Begotten of the Father before all worlds; God, of God; Light, of Light; Very God of very God; Begotten, not made; Being of one substance with the Father: Through whom all things were made: Who for us men and for our Salvation came down from heaven, And was incarnate by the Holy Spirit of the Virgin Mary, And was made man: And was crucified also for us under Pontius Pilate; He suffered and was buried: And the Third day he rose again according to the Scriptures: And ascended into heaven, And sit at the right hand of the Father: And he shall come again, with glory, to judge both the living and the dead; Whose kingdom shall have no end

And I believe in the Holy Spirit, The Lord, the giver of life, who proceeds from the Father and the Son; who with the Father and the Son is worshipped and glorified; who spoke by the prophets. And I believe one Holy Catholic and Apostolic Church: I acknowledge one Baptism for the remission of Sins: And I look for the Resurrection of the dead: And the life of the world to come. Amen.

When there is no Communion, the Apostles' Creed may be used instead.

The Intercession

The Intercession may be led by a layman. The Minister may use any or all of the following petitions and add others at his discretion.

The Minister says:
Let us pray for the whole Church of Christ and for all men according to their needs.

The people kneel, and after each petition answer:
Hear us, good Lord.

On weekdays, the following prayer may be used instead.

O God, the Creator and Preserver of all mankind, we humbly beseech thee for all sorts and conditions of men; that thou wouldest be pleased to make thy ways known unto them, thy saving health unto all nations. More especially we pray for the good estate of the Catholic Church; that it may be so guided and

For the saving knowledge of thyself, and for thy divine grace, we pray to thee, O God:

For the union of all Christians in one holy Church, we pray to thee, O God:

For all Bishops, Priests, and Deacons, and especially for thy servant N. our Bishop, we pray to thee, O God:

For Catechists, Readers, and all other servants of the Church, we pray to thee, O God:

For the peace of the whole world, we pray to thee, O God:

For the just government of all nations in accordance with thy holy will, we pray to thee, O God:

For the rulers of our country (especially . . . Head of State) and for all who are in authority over us, we pray to thee, O God:

For doctors and nurses, and all who serve the sick, we pray to thee, O God:

For teachers and those who influence others by their words, we pray to thee, O God:

For all men and women in their daily work, we pray to thee, O God:

For our homes and all parents and children, we pray to thee, O God:

For those who travel by land, air, or water, we pray to thee, O God:

For the conversion of those in governed by thy good Spirit, that all who profess and call themselves Christians may be led into the way of truth, and hold the faith in unity of spirit, in the bond of peace, and in righteousness of life. And we commend to thy fatherly goodness all those who are any way afflicted or distressed in mind, body, or estate; that it may please thee to comfort and relieve them, according to their several necessities, giving them patience under their sufferings, and a happy issue out of all their afflictions. And we also bless thy holy name for all thy servants departed this life in thy faith and fear, beseeching thee that with them we may be partakers of thy heavenly kingdom; through Jesus Christ our Lord. **Amen.**

unbelief and error, we pray to
thee, O God:

For favourable weather for our
crops, we pray to thee, O God:

For the poor and hungry, the
homeless and unemployed, we
pray to thee, O God:

For the lonely and oppressed,
we pray to thee, O God:

For those who suffer
persecution, we pray to thee,
O God:

For the sick and suffering in
mind or body, we pray to thee,
O God:

For the sorrowful and the dying,
we pray to thee, O God:

For all who have departed this
life in thy faith and fear, we
pray to thee, O God:

Hasten, O Father, the coming of
thy kingdom; and grant that we
and all thy servants, walking in
new life and in the eternal
fellowship of thy Holy Spirit, may
with joy behold thy Son at his
coming in glorious majesty, even
Jesus Christ, our only Mediator
and Advocate. Amen.

If the Service of the Lord's Supper follows, all may say this prayer:

We do not presume to come to this thy Table, O merciful Father, trusting
in our own righteousness, but in thy manifold and great mercies. We are
not worthy so much as to gather up the crumbs under thy Table. But thou
art the same Lord, whose mercy never fails. Grant us, therefore, gracious
Lord, so to eat the Flesh of thy dear Son Jesus Christ, and to drink his
Blood, that we being cleansed in body and soul may evermore dwell in him
and he in us. Amen.

If there is no celebration of the Lord's Supper a hymn is sung. Then the alms are brought to the Minister. He places them on the Lord's Table and says:

Thine, O Lord, is the greatness and the power and the glory and the majesty.

And the people answer:

All that is in the heaven and the earth is thine, and of thine own do we give to thee.

Almighty God, Father of all mercies, we thine unworthy servants do give thee most humble and hearty thanks for all thy goodness and loving-kindness to us and to all men. We bless thee for our creation, preservation, and all the blessings of this life; but above all for thine inestimable love in the redemption of the world by our Lord Jesus Christ, for the means of grace and for the hope of glory. And we beseech thee, give us that due sense of all thy mercies, that our hearts may be unfeignedly thankful, and that we show forth thy praise, not only with our lips, but in our lives: by giving up ourselves to thy service, and by walking before thee in holiness and righteousness all our days; through Jesus Christ our Lord, to whom with thee and the Holy Spirit be all honour and glory, world without end. Amen.

Our Father, who art in heaven, hallowed be thy Name, thy kingdom come, thy will be done, in earth as it is in heaven. Give us this day our daily bread: and forgive us our trespasses, as we forgive them that trespass against us: and lead us not into temptation, but deliver us from evil. For thine is the kingdom, the power, and the glory, for ever and ever. Amen.

The grace of our Lord Jesus Christ, the love of God, and the fellowship of the Holy Spirit, be with us all evermore. Amen.

The Service of the Lord's Supper

A hymn may be sung. The gifts of the people and the bread and wine for Communion are made ready for bringing to the Lord's Table.

THE PEACE

The Priest turns to the people and says:

The Peace of the Lord be always with you.

And the people answer:

And with thy spirit.

Or the Priest may touch hands with those in the Sanctuary, saying the same words, and they in turn may pass the greeting in like manner to the people.

THE PLACING OF THE GIFTS

The gifts of the people and the bread and wine are brought to the Minister, who places them upon the Lord's Table and says:

Thine, O Lord, is the greatness and the power and the glory and the majesty.

And the people answer:

All that is in the heaven and the earth is thine, and of thine own do we give to thee.

THE GREAT THANKSGIVING

Lift up your hearts.
We lift them up unto the Lord.
Let us give thanks unto the Lord, our God.
It is meet and right so to do.

It is most meet and right that we should at all times and in all places give thanks unto thee, O Lord, Holy Father, Almighty, Everlasting God, through Jesus Christ our Lord, through whom thou hast made and dost sustain the worlds. We praise thee for the order of thy creation, and for all the material blessings of our life.

But chiefly we praise thee for thy love for fallen man in giving thy Son to take our nature upon him, to die for our sins and to be raised from the dead for our justification. We praise thee, O God, who hast set him in glory at thy right hand, where he ever lives to make intercession for us, who draw near to thee through him.

Again, we praise thee, O Father, for sending to us the promised Holy Spirit, through whom thou dost pour out upon us thy manifold gifts of grace and hast made us a royal priesthood, to set forth thy praises who hast called us out of darkness into the glory of thy light.

Therefore with angels and archangels, with patriarchs and prophets, apostles and martyrs, and with all the holy company of heaven, we cry aloud with joy, evermore praising thee and saying:

Holy, Holy, Holy, Lord God of hosts, heaven and earth are full of thy glory. Glory be to thee, O Lord most high.

All glory be to thee, O heavenly Father, who in thy tender mercy didst give thine only Son Jesus Christ that all who believe in him might have eternal life. Hear us, O merciful Father, we humbly beseech thee, and grant that we receiving this Bread and this Cup, in remembrance of the death and passion of thy Son our Saviour Jesus Christ, may be partakers of his most blessed Body and Blood: for in the same night that he gave himself to death, he took Bread, and when he had given thanks to thee he broke it and gave it to his disciples, saying, Take, eat, this is my Body which is given for you, do this in remembrance of me. Likewise after supper he took the Cup, and when he had given thanks to thee he gave it to them, saying, Drink this, all of you, for this is my Blood of the New Covenant which is shed for you and for many, for the remission of sins, do this as often as you drink it, in remembrance of me.

His death, O Father, we proclaim. His resurrection we confess. His coming we await. Glory to thee, O Lord.

Wherefore, O Father, we do this as thy Son commanded, offering to thee, with this holy Bread and Cup, our praise and thanksgiving for his one sacrifice once offered upon the cross, for his mighty resurrection and glorious ascension. Accept us in him, we beseech thee, and grant that all we who are partakers of this holy communion may be filled with thy Holy Spirit and made one in thy holy Church, the body of thy Son Jesus Christ our Lord, through whom and in whom, in the unity of the Holy Spirit, all honour and glory be to thee, O Father Almighty, for ever and ever. Amen.

As our Saviour Christ has taught us, we say:

Our Father, who art in heaven, hallowed be thy Name, thy kingdom come, thy will be done, in earth as it is in heaven. Give us this day our daily bread: and forgive us our trespasses, as we forgive them that trespass against us: and lead us not into temptation, but deliver us from evil. For thine is the kingdom, the power, and the glory, for ever and ever. Amen.

THE BREAKING OF THE BREAD

After a short silence the Priest breaks the Bread, saying:

The Bread which we break, is it not a sharing of the Body of Christ?
We who are many are one body, for we all partake of the one loaf.

THE COMMUNION

Then the Priest receives the Holy Communion himself, and afterwards ministers it to the congregation, first saying:

Draw near and receive the Body and Blood of our Lord Jesus Christ, which were given for you, and feed on him in your hearts by faith with thanksgiving.

When he delivers the Bread to any one, he says:

The Body of our Lord Jesus Christ, which was given for thee. **Amen.**

And when he delivers the Cup, he says:

The Blood of our Lord Jesus Christ, which was shed for thee. **Amen.**

If any of the consecrated Elements remain, the Ministers reverently consume them when all have received Communion or immediately after the Dismissal.

THE DISMISSAL

Silence is kept for a space, while all make their thanksgiving to God. Then the Priest says:

O give thanks unto the Lord, for he is gracious.
And his mercy endureth for ever.

Then is said:

Bless the Lord, O my soul, and all that is within me, bless his holy name;
Bless the Lord, O my soul, and forget not all his benefits;

Who forgives all your iniquity,
Who heals all your diseases,
Who redeems your life from destruction,
Who crowns you with steadfast love and mercy,
Who satisfies you with good as long as you live,
So that your youth is renewed like the eagle's.
Bless the Lord, all his works, in all places of his dominion,
Bless the Lord, O my soul.
Glory be to the Father, and to the Son, and to the Holy Ghost;
As it was in the beginning, is now, and ever shall be, world without end.
  Amen.

Gloria in excelsis *or* Te Deum (*from the sentence: Thou art the King of glory, O Christ*), *or* Nunc Dimittis, *or another Psalm may be used instead of the above Psalm 103.*

The Priest says this or another prayer:

Holy Father, we beseech thee to keep in thy truth all whom thou hast made one in thy Son our Saviour Jesus Christ. Grant us strength and power through thy spirit in our inner being, that we may keep our eyes fixed on the hope that thou dost set before us, and walk worthily of our calling. Make us faithful in our witness and constant in our service. Help us to meet whatever comes with fortitude, patience, and joy, to the praise and glory of thy holy name, through the same thy Son, Jesus Christ our Lord. Amen.

> The Lord be with you.
> **And with thy spirit.**
> Go forth in the name of the Lord
> **Thanks be to God.**

If the consecrated Bread be finished before all have communicated, the Priest is to consecrate more, saying:

Holy art thou, O Father, and worthy to receive blessing and honour and glory; for that thou didst send thy Son our Saviour Jesus Christ, who in the same night that he gave himself to death took Bread, and when he had given thanks he broke it and gave it to his disciples, saying, Take, eat, this is my Body which is given for you, do this in remembrance of me.

If more Wine is to be consecrated, the Priest says:

Holy art thou, O Father, and worthy to receive blessing and honour and glory; for that thou didst send thy Son our Saviour Jesus Christ, who in the same night that he gave himself to death after supper took the Cup, and when he had given thanks he gave it to them, saying, Drink this, all of you, for this is my Blood of the New Covenant which is shed for you and for many, for the remission of sins, do this as often as you drink it, in remembrance of me.

PRAYERS
which may be used in the Dismissal

GENERAL

Almighty and Everlasting God, we most heartily thank thee for graciously feeding us, in these holy mysteries, with the spiritual food of the most precious Body and Blood of thy Son Jesus Christ, assuring us thereby of thy favour and goodness towards us; and that we are living members of his mystical body and are also heirs through hope of thy eternal kingdom. Here we offer and present to thee, O Lord, ourselves, our souls and bodies, to be a reasonable, holy, and living sacrifice unto thee. And although we are unworthy, yet we beseech thee to accept this our bounden duty and sacrifice, not weighing our merits, but pardoning our offences, through Jesus Christ our Lord, to whom, with thee and the Holy Spirit, be all honour and glory for ever. **Amen.**

Remember, O Lord, what thou hast wrought in us and not what we deserve; and as thou hast called us to thy service, make us worthy of our calling; through Jesus Christ our Lord, who liveth and reigneth with thee in the unity of the Holy Spirit, ever one God, world without end. **Amen.**

Grant us, O Lord, not to mind earthly things, but to love things heavenly; and, while we sojourn among things that are passing away, to cleave to these that shall abide; through Jesus Christ our Lord, who liveth and reigneth with thee in the unity of the Holy Spirit, ever one God, world without end. **Amen.**

ADVENT

Grant, O Almighty God, that as thy blessed Son Jesus Christ at his first advent came to seek and to save that which was lost, so at his second and glorious appearing he may find in us the fruits of the redemption which he wrought; who liveth and reigneth, with thee and the Holy Spirit, one God, world without end. **Amen.**

CHRISTMAS DAY
until the eve of the Epiphany, inclusive

O Merciful Jesus, who, when thou tookest upon thee to deliver man, didst not abhor the Virgin's womb: vouchsafe evermore to dwell in the hearts of us thy servants; inspire us with thy purity; strengthen us with thy might; make us perfect in thy ways; guide us into thy truth; and unite us to thyself and to thy whole Church by thy holy mysteries; that we may conquer every adverse power, and may be wholly devoted to thy service and conformed to thy will; to the glory of God the Father. **Amen.**

THE EPIPHANY
and seven days after

Almighty and Everlasting God, who didst bring the nations to thy light and kings to the brightness of thy rising: fill, we pray thee, the world with thy glory, and show thyself unto all mankind, through him who is the true Light, the bright and morning star, even thy Son Jesus Christ our Lord, who liveth and reigneth with thee and the Holy Spirit, ever one God, world without end. **Amen.**

ASH WEDNESDAY
until the Saturday before Passion Sunday, inclusive

O God, whose nature and property is ever to have mercy and to forgive: receive our humble petitions; and though we be tied and bound with the chain of our sins, yet let the pitifulness of thy great mercy loose us; for the honour of Jesus Christ, our Mediator and Advocate, who liveth and reigneth with thee in the unity of the Holy Spirit, ever one God, world without end. **Amen.**

PASSION SUNDAY
until Maundy Thursday, inclusive

O God, whose blessed Son did overcome death for our salvation: mercifully grant that we who have his glorious passion in remembrance may take up our cross daily and follow him; through the same Jesus Christ our Lord, who liveth and reigneth with thee, in the unity of the Holy Spirit, ever one God, world without end. **Amen.**

EASTER DAY
until the eve of the Ascension, inclusive

O God, who for our redemption didst give thine only-begotten Son to the death of the cross, and by his glorious resurrection hast delivered us from the power of our enemy: grant us so to die daily unto sin, that we may evermore live with him in the joy of his resurrection; through the same Jesus Christ our Lord, who liveth and reigneth with thee in the unity of the Holy Spirit, ever one God, world without end. **Amen.**

ASCENSION DAY
until the eve of Whitsun, inclusive

O God, whose blessed Son did as at this time ascend unto the throne of thy majesty in heaven: grant that, as he reigneth in glory at thy right hand, so he may be enthroned in the hearts of us thy servants, who, with thee and the Holy Spirit, liveth and reigneth ever one God, world without end. **Amen.**

WHITSUN
and six days after

O Almighty God, who on the day of Pentecost didst send the Holy Spirit the Comforter to abide in thy Church for ever: bestow upon us his manifold gifts of grace, that, enlightened by his truth and purified by his presence, we may daily be strengthened with his power; through Jesus Christ, our Lord, who liveth and reigneth with thee and the same Spirit, ever one God, world without end. **Amen.**

SAINTS' DAYS

O God, the King of Saints, we praise and magnify thy holy name for all thy servants who have finished their course in thy faith and fear; and we beseech thee that, encouraged by their example, and aided by their prayers, we may at length enjoy their company in the eternal gladness; through the merits of thy Son Jesus Christ our Lord, who liveth and reigneth with thee and the Holy Spirit, one God, world without end. **Amen.**

THE FEAST OF THE DEDICATION OF A CHURCH

O God, who hast brought us again to the feast of the dedication of this thy holy temple, and dost allow us to present ourselves in safety at thy holy mysteries: hear the prayers of thy people, and grant that whosoever shall enter this temple to ask thy blessing, may rejoice that he has gained all his petitions; through Jesus Christ our Lord, who liveth and reigneth with thee in the unity of the Holy Spirit, ever one God, world without end. **Amen.**